The Actor's Picture/Resume Book

*An actor's guide
to creating a picture/resume
for theatre, film and commercials.*

by Jill Charles

with Tom Bloom

Published by Theatre Directories,
a program of American Theatre Works, Inc.
Dorset, Vermont

ISBN 0-933919-18-2

Publisher: Theatre Directories, a program of American Theatre Works, Inc.;
P.O. Box 519, Dorset, Vermont 05251 (802) 867-2223

Set in 12 point New Century Schoolbook, on Xerox Ventura Publisher™
Printed at Lamb Printing, North Adams, Mass.

Manufactured in the United States of America.

Printed on recycled paper.

Other Publications from Theatre Directories:

Regional Theatre Directory
Jobs & Internships at 430 Regional & Dinner Theatres

Summer Theatre Directory
450 Summer Theatres & Summer Training Programs

Directory of Theatre Training Programs
Programs at 400 Colleges, Universities, & Conservatories

Auditions & Scenes from Shakespeare
Guide to over 700 Selections, for 1 – 5 Actors

Showbiz Bookkeeper
Tax Record-Keeping System for Professionals in the Arts

for more information or to order books:
THEATRE DIRECTORIES
P.O. Box 519, Dorset, VT 05251
☎ *802-867-2223;* © *802-867-0144*

*This book is dedicated to Michael D'Apice,
a gifted artist and wonderful friend,
who left us far too early.*

Special Thanks:

Donna Fumoso, make-up and hair styling, and excellent advice.
Toni Weissman, retouching, and excellent advice.
Scott Hopper, Deborah Mendel, Michelle Ortlip, Peter Principato,
Mark Ramont, Jean Rohn, Barry Shapiro and Anne Stein, for their
excellent advice as casting directors and agents.
All the generous actors and actresses who allowed us to use their photos as
illustrations: John Beuscher, Ron Brown, Stewart Burney, Tony Capone,
Gráinne Cassidy, Jill Christenson, Cate Damon, Maia DeSanti, Peter Fletcher,
Jim Grollman, Jesse Holmes, Jennifer Jacoby, Bruce Katlin, Keshia Korman,
Charlotte Lopez, Laura MacDermott, Kathleen Mulligan, Libby Page,
Jayne Ross, Tracy Sallows, Andrea Savage, William Sharp, Sharon Stone,
Terry Sweeney, Lisa Wingate.
(Also Barbara Gulan and Ted Anderson, even though we didn't use
their pictures after all!)
Bob and Kenny Lamb, printers extraordinaire.

About the Authors...

**Jill Charles** has served as Artistic Director of the Dorset Theatre Festival for 20 years, and in that time has looked at approximately 40,000 Picture/ Resumes. She has directed over 50 productions, and has taught in both conservatory and liberal arts settings. She created and continues to edit the *Summer* and *Regional Theatre Directories*, employment guides covering a total of 850 professional theatres across the U.S., and the national *Directory of Theatre Training Programs*. She has written feature articles for *Back Stage* and *Dramatics* on pictures & resumes, auditioning, selecting a training program, regional theatres and various other topics.

**Tom Bloom** has combined the worlds of theatre and photography professionally for 21 years. He has photographed productions and advertising for most of the principal theatre, opera and dance companies in New England, and his studio became the best known theatrical portrait studio in Boston. Living in new York since 1984, Tom maintains his photography studio while also working professionally as an actor and director. Regional and Off-Broadway appearances have included roles at Circle in the Square, Playwrights' Horizons, Soho Rep, Manhattan Theatre Club, Lincoln Center, Indiana Rep and Capital Rep as well as many other companies in Boston and New England.

TABLE OF CONTENTS

Photo A - *Portrait style, shot to the elbow. Notice the importance of the eyes which draw in the viewer.*

Photo B - *Portrait style, to below the waist. The eyes become less important as the size of the face is reduced; the impact is more from the overall face and body posture.*

Photo C - *Another example of a portrait style photo "to the table," where the eyes still play an important part, but enough body shows to add interest and more personality.*

Photo D - *Portrait style to below the waist, again emphasizing the overall person. Eyes are active but not predominant.*

Introduction to the Third Printing

Since this book was first published in 1991, Tom Bloom and I have gotten a lot of good feedback on it. When we realized we had to go to a third printing, we reviewed the book to see if we felt any changes were necessary. We came up with only one issue—photo styles—which we decided to deal with in this new Introduction with a few additional pictures (opposite) as illustration.

As I explain at the beginning of Chapter 2, in the spring of 1991, about 80-90% of the picture/resumes found at New York auditions were the traditional borderless headshots; the remaining 10-20% were what we call "portrait" shots, showing more than the actor's head, with a wide white border and thin black line separating the border from the photo. However, in the three years since our first printing, the ratio has changed significantly, so that now probably 50-60% of the shots coming across a casting table are the portrait style. They may include anything from head and shoulders, to head and torso, to three-quarters or full body.

In 1991 several theatrical casting directors I spoke to liked the portrait style, but several commercial people indicated they still wanted head-shots. That seems to have changed, judging from recent conversations with Peter Principato, a commercial talent agent at the William Morris Agency, and Barry Shapiro, a commercial casting director with Herman & Lipson Casting. Both liked the portrait style because it gave a better indication of body type. Peter said he looks for something more interesting that a standard headshot, and feels the wide white border focuses attention on the actor more than a head-shot does. Barry suggests that someone in their 20's or 30's ("the type who might be Levi's material," as he said) who thinks their body will help sell them should probably show more body, perhaps as much as three-quarters, while an older actor may prefer to emphasize the face and eyes with a headshot.

I asked Tom what changes he had experienced in the last three years as a photographer, and he agreed that more and more people are asking for the portrait style; in fact, he estimates that 80-90% of his clients are going away with some combination that includes at least one portrait style. He explained that while some actors are under the illusion that certain photographers do that style and others don't, in actuality any good photographer should be able to do both headshot and portrait. Tom urges actors to ask photographers if they do both; technically, it's not a big deal at all, just a matter of being able to pull the camera back about four or five feet. Some photographers might hedge your question because they don't have the studio set up with a background that's large enough for a longer shot. If you know you want portrait style, look for examples of it when you go through a prospective photographer's book.

How much body should you include? Well, it seems now that almost anything goes in terms of what will be acceptable in the industry, so the decision you need to make is how important you want the face and eyes to be in a particular shot. Tom explains that he now always shoots "down to the table;" that is, including the head, shoulders and arms down to the elbow, assuming the subject is leaning on a table. Hands may be relaxed down along the table, folded, or with one or both up to the face, but the amount of body seen is from head to elbow. From this, he can crop to a simple headshot if that is desired, without losing quality. But if he shoots any further down than the elbow, the shot can't be blown up to head alone without becoming too grainy to be acceptable.

If a client desires more body shown, Tom will pull back even further, to include to the waist, or three-quarter or full, perhaps with the subject leaning against a wall or sitting on a stool. But one must remember that the further back the camera is, the less important the face becomes, and thus the eyes play a lesser role. We have included four new photos in this reprint which illustrate how the length of the shot affects the size of the face and the impact of the eyes (see photos A–D, opposite the previous page).

Tom told me he likes shooting the longer shot because it tends to help the subject relax more. "Something happens in the session," he says, "when you know you're being shot up tight, and there's a greater scrutiny on your face. But when you know it's your whole body, you're more willing to break the line and animate the body."

One result of shooting lower than the shoulders is that more background shows, which has led many studios to make use of textured or mottled backgrounds. Tom objected to backgrounds with too much motion, feeling that it will dilute the power of the eyes of the subject. He explains, "whenever I look at a picture like that and I hear people commenting on the background first, that strikes me as too much of the photographer's 'signature'—it's as if a director were to come on stage with the actors. I think the background should be more neutral."

Rules are relaxing a bit in clothing, Tom felt, advising that "if there's something you love that breaks the rules, try it—as long as it's not overpowering." He cited as example an actress who brought in a denim vest that had brocade and sequins all over it, which resulted in a striking photo. Speaking of denim, though, the standard issue jean jacket seems to have reached its limit; Tom feels it's been done to death, and suggests giving it a rest. Otherwise, the discussions in the following chapters on hair, clothing and make-up still hold.

Prices have gone up since our first printing (surprise, surprise), with make-up artists now costing about $135 to do a shoot with 2-3 hair and make-up changes. However, there are some good make-up studios in New York, where you can go to have your make-up done before a shoot for about $75. Obviously, you would have to do any changes in hair or make-up yourself for different types of shots. The going rate for the photo session now starts at about $245, and may go as high as $500, including make-up and hair. You will generally be offered one or two prints for the base price, with 'extras' adding to the cost.

Whether you're new at the business or an old hand, we hope this book will save you time, energy and money in helping you put together a P/R that works *for* you, and gets you noticed by agents and casting people.

Jill Charles & Tom Bloom
Dorset, Vermont, 1994

Chapter 1

A Picture/Resume: The Actor's Calling Card

At times I wonder what kind of a business we've created where people need a book to tell them how to package an image of themselves that is going to attract the attention of an agent who will try to sell that image to a casting director who will try to sell that image to a director as *the* image needed to do anything from selling a lite beer to keeping 40 million viewers glued to the tube or even bringing an audience to tears and cheers in a real live play. Be that as it may, you who are reading this, presumably, are actors, and if you're experiencing similar qualms I trust you will ignore them long enough to get through this book. Having read it, you should be able to hold your own at that photo session that's going to cost you half a month's rent.

Before getting into specifics about photos and resumes, let's talk concepts. We all know that a Picture/Resume won't get you a part; only you, at your audition, can get you a part. But your P/R can get you the audition, and that's the first step. A P/R could be compared to a business card, since it represents your contact with your profession, but it has to do much more than any normal business card. A business person hands out a card once someone has taken an interest in her business. Your P/R has to *create* an interest in your business, that is, *in you*. And it has to do this in competition with, not half a dozen other business cards the prospective client has collected, but hundreds of other actors pursuing the same objective.

So we'll say that essentially a good P/R must *create an interest* in the eye and mind of the viewer—he must *want to see the person* behind the image in the photo and described on the resume. Let me illustrate this by explaining how one director (me) uses pictures and resumes in casting a show. I'm quick to admit that this may not be the way all directors do it (in fact, who knows, I may be the only director in the world who does it this way), but since it's a good illustration I'll use it, nonetheless.

Many of the calls my casting director puts out for auditions will be to people whose work I have seen, or with whom I've worked before. But perhaps a third of the actors called in for any role will be coming in "cold," on the basis of a picture and resume received directly from them by mail, or through an agent's submission. I'm casting a summer season of five plays with a total of 20-25 characters to be cast, and to set up auditions I'll probably have to look through three or four hundred P/R's of actors with whom I'm completely unfamiliar. I'll audition a total of about 15 for each role, so we'll say 10 known and five unknown, which means 75 people will be called in from those "cold" P/R's.

Here's how I do it. *Step one:* the P/R's are sorted by sex and age appropriate to the role being cast. *Step two:* I flip through this pile, looking only at the photo, and pull out all the ones that, on the basis of their photo, I could envision playing the role. *Step three:* I turn that pile over and look at the resumes, to eliminate those who, in my judgment, don't have enough experience, or the right kind of experience for the role (for example, if it's a wild farce, I might eliminate someone whose credits are all classical drama). This usually leaves me with a pile of P/R's that is still too large for the number of audition slots I have available, so I go on to the crucial *Step four:* I lay out the photos on the floor, usually about twelve at a time (three neat rows of four photos each), and stand back and look at them all. I pull out the one or two (or three, or five) that jump out at me, that really look like they have the potential to make the character I'm trying to cast come to life. I set them aside and lay out the next 12, and so on until I have selected the actors who will be called in to audition. As I'm making this final cut I will turn to the resume again, especially on close calls, weighing the actors' credits as well as their look. If at the end of step four I still have more P/R's than audition slots, I'll simply repeat the step, being even more stringent (an actor would probably say "hardhearted") this time.

Now, what control does the actor have in this process? Not much when it comes to sex and age, obviously. And of course my conception of how the character should look is entirely subjective; another director casting the same play might pull an entirely different set of pictures. And yet, step two is where the strength of a good headshot and resume begins to come into play, because while I may have a specific idea about a look, even at this stage I will be influenced, positively or negatively, by the overall impression of a P/R. If a photo looks unprofessional, if features are hidden by shadow, if a resume is too crowded or badly typed with extra credits scribbled in, these read as negatives and I'm less likely to pull that P/R. You can't control how I see the character, but you *can* present yourself in a positive light, which will improve your odds significantly.

If you get through the first cut, what will make your photo jump out at me from the dozen I have laid out on the floor? Step four is where the quality of your headshot will make or break you: the essence that reaches out of the photo and draws me in, that says "I've got something to show you—call me in so you can see it in person." It is the *potential* that I see in a P/R that gets the actor an audition. Now take this one step further, to the actual audition. Having called in an actor on the basis of what I saw in her P/R, what happens if the actor who comes to audition is not the person the photo led me to expect? Obviously it's a disappointment and a waste of time for both of us, and it will work against our establishing a professional relationship in the future.

"So," you're saying, "a good photo and resume is important—tell me something I *didn't* know. But how do I guarantee that the photo I'm going to ransom my first-born to pay for is going to be a good one?" By reading the rest of this book, wherein a photographer/director/actor spills all his trade secrets. I've watched Tom Bloom during a photo shoot and observed how he *directs* an actor into revealing her uniqueness to the camera. I believe Tom's approach will help any actor to first find a good photographer and then get a theatrical photo that *works*.

What Your P/R Must Do For You

Remember as you go through this book the importance of creating a tool that will work *for* you. If your P/R doesn't serve you well (or rather, brilliantly), you've done worse than waste your money—you've spent all that money to sabotage your career. As an actor you have a number of tools available to you to pry open the door to an audition that could lead to a job: your P/R, your agent, your contacts, your training, etc. If any one of those tools is not working very hard *for* you, then it's working against you, and you'd better do something about it, quick. Remember the moment in *A Chorus Line* when the dancers all hold their headshots up in front of their faces? Well the real question isn't "Am I my resume?" but rather "Is my photo me?" ***If your photo doesn't project your uniqueness, and if it doesn't look the way you do when you walk in the door, then you've paid someone a lot of money to obstruct your career.***

To look like you, your photo must reflect more than your physical attributes, it must reflect the life inside you. A good photo should have an immediacy; the sense that the actor is *including* the viewer. Your photo should be *you* specifically, not a generic type of actor. Remember you're selling yourself, not a type or range (this is not to say, however, that you shouldn't *know* your general type or range). The picture should embody your real sparkle, where your center is; it should emphasize your uniqueness, what makes you different from all the other actors. Your photo must reflect in two dimensions the *presence* that you have onstage as an actor.

Variations on the above theme will be repeated *ad nauseam* in this book. I will go to great lengths turning semantic handsprings trying to come up with new ways of phrasing it, but there it is: the inner, special *you* must come out in your picture, or you will not be called in to the audition to show it in person. This book can teach you to put together a good resume, one that looks professional and shows you off to your best advantage; the photographic illustrations can show you technical problems to avoid and we can give you a technique to use which should prepare you for a productive photo session. But *you* have the ultimate task (think of it as an acting objective if you like) to allow *yourself* to come through in front of that lens.

Tom's approach to this task when he works with an actor is to direct the actor toward *including* the camera at the shooting session, as opposed to simply *looking at* the camera. The resulting photograph is one that *invites* the viewer to come in and share something with the actor. Essentially, Tom directs the actor in a mini scene in which *he or she has a secret and is about to include the observer in that secret*. This makes for a sense of involvement and of mystery; it serves to draw the viewer into the scene. Much more about this technique when we get to the chapter on the actual shooting session, but keep this concept in mind.

About Agents...

We've written this book with the assumption that you're doing this on your own, and don't have an agent yet. Once you do have an agent, s/he will advise you on your P/R, based on her/his own experience with the business and her/his preferences when it comes to selling clients to casting people. This is a double-edged sword. It's great to have someone on your team to help you develop the most effective P/R you can, and one that you both feel is a good business tool. It's not so great if your new agent says you have to throw out the P/R you just spent two months and $600 on—the one that got you this agent in the first place—and start all over. Remember one thing: your agent works for you, not the other way around. You should be able to discuss your P/R with your agent, and get a reasonable, constructive critique of how well, in her/his opinion, it works for you. If s/he has criticisms which appear valid, listen to her/him; on the other hand, if you believe it would be a waste of *your* money to redo your P/R's, then s/he will just have to live with them until *you* decide it's time to redo them. Be very wary if an agent seems to be pushing a certain photographer at you, or if an agent says you must have photographer X do your photos as a condition of signing with that agency. This is completely unethical and the agency could be in big trouble if collusion is discovered between an agent and a photographer. Of course, agents can (and should) recommend photographers that they feel are good and have done well by other clients of theirs. But a hard sell or outright demand that you work with a particular photographer should have you running to Equity or SAG to investigate the agency's franchise.

When it comes to the resume, you may find an agent has certain preferences as to how it's laid out and what information you include. Since the resume is a much less expensive proposition than the photo, it's generally simple to comply. But I offer a *caveat* here, too. I have been astonished at some of the *awful* resumes that have been submitted to me by agents. They have been badly typed, badly copied, on paper larger or smaller than the photo and not attached to it; some have had very little information on actors I knew had a great deal of experience, and others were so full you couldn't read them, especially with all the credits hand-written in. The point is, even when you have an agent, your P/R is still your own responsibility. Come to an agreement with your agent as to how it will look, and keep it accurately updated. Check in frequently with your agent to be sure s/he has plenty of copies of your most recent P/R (and see that s/he destroys the old ones!) Many times I've had an actor come into an audition, see the P/R I have in my hand, turn pale and ask me "Where did you get *that*?" Sometimes it's been kicking around in my own files for three years, but just as often it was sent over by the agency yesterday.

I will end with this: many actors tend to be uneasy about the business aspect of their career, and hence are very easily intimidated by people like photographers and agents who seem to have all the answers. They don't have all the answers for your career because ultimately they're more interested in their own. *You* are the only one who is more interested in yours. You hire these people to perform services for you because you think their expertise will be useful to you. You don't give over your life into their hands to do with as they will. *You* make your own decisions after listening carefully to the expert advice of those whose services you've hired; if you don't trust their advice, you hire someone else's services. If you don't feel you have the business acumen or knowledge of the industry to make your own decisions, then *you must acquire those skills*, rather than continuing to blindly put your career in the hands of those you hire. A *good* agent will agree with this concept, and will, in fact, encourage it in your working relationship.

Chapter 2

Style

Picture/Resumes, like most things, have styles that come and go and shift and change, so that a P/R from ten years ago looks as out of date as bell bottoms. Fashion and personal taste will dictate such things as whether one uses a headshot, a 3/4 body shot or something in between; whether a photo is bordered or borderless, with a glossy, pearl or matte finish. Now if, as I am preaching, a good photograph is one that reveals the inner you while actively including the viewer, then shouldn't that factor override fashion? Why should one worry about style?

Ultimately, what works best for you and what you feel comfortable with is the arbiter of *your* style. But there is a strong argument for being aware of current styles in P/R's and striving to fall within those parameters: it is essential that your P/R project your professionalism. Indeed, many actors feel it speaks to their being a *working* actor to keep up to date on the latest fashion in P/R's. And there are some subtle reasons for new styles working their way into the business, which have to do with changing attitudes of casting people, which are in turn reflections of changing attitudes in Madison Avenue, Hollywood, and maybe even our society at large. For instance, the formality or casualness of photos will change with the tenor of the times, as might the trend toward "up-scale" or "laid-back."

This does not mean you have to change your photos every spring and fall like designer clothes, because P/R styles tend to change slowly, and in a fairly nebulous flow. What it does mean is that when you decide to have a new picture done, rather than automatically reshooting what you did last time, look around and see if styles have changed any. You can do that fairly easily, just by taking a close look at as many P/R's as you can find for a couple of weeks, and by asking around among other actors, directors and casting people. You will probably get a variety of opinions, but knowing what's floating around out there will help you determine the approach that's best for you. The observations made in this book reflect the current styles of Spring 1991; if things change a lot in three years or so, we'll update with a new edition (or maybe sooner if this printing sells out, so tell your friends to buy this book).

New York, NY, *To*tally L.A. or like, Bicoastal, Dude?

Ten years ago the standard theatrical photo was a glossy headshot with a 3/8" white border. This gradually shifted to what is now the NYC standard: a black and white studio headshot, borderless with a matte or pearl finish, with the actor's name printed on the front. This is the style represented in most of the photos in this book because it's still pretty much the standard across the country in theatre and commercials. Also, it offers the best opportunity to focus on the life in the subjects' faces and to understand exactly what points are strong or weak about a particular photo.

Currently the trend in L.A. seems to be moving away from the standard headshot to something more full-bodied, casual, and with that "L.A. feel." In looking at a stack of P/R's from the west coast clients of some agents, the distinction from the typical NYC headshot was striking. The L.A. pictures showed the subjects to the waist or full figure, in casual poses, most taken outdoors in natural lighting, printed without a border. The backgrounds, thrown out of focus, were trees, a big rock, the wall of a building, etc. The photos were asymmetrical, with the face off center. One actor's photo was cropped from head to hips, with the line of the actor's body across the page on an asymmetrical diagonal, as if he were leaning or walking out of the frame; in fact, some of his hair was cut off by the upper right corner. Another was of an actress sitting on a rock in a shot which included the whole body and a good deal of background; as a result her face was reduced to only a few square inches in the photo. In general, they reminded me of those full page fashion ads in the NY Times magazine where you look at the ad and have no idea whether they're trying to sell jeans, shoes or cosmetics, but they obviously used a very expensive photographer. However, it occurs to me that this trend to the more full-body, outdoor pose is an attempt to plant an actor's "image" in the mind of the casting person, rather than to emphasize the details of his/her visage. And this makes sense, I suppose, when casting for film and TV; the primary concern may be finding an actor with a particular image.

A third style of photo, which falls somewhere between headshot and the L.A. look, has been turning up in New York this spring—we'll refer to it as the "portrait style" photo. Some of these are shot outdoors, but most are studio shots, and they include a portion of the torso, perhaps down to the waist, with arms and hands in view, or sometimes a full body shot as in the L.A. style. Rather than "bleeding," or completely filling the 8"x10" photo paper, you will see a white border, usually wider on the sides than on top and bottom, and often with an uneven black line around the photographic image.

Now please bear with me as we take a slight sidetrack for a technical explanation of these shots. As you may or may not know, a 35mm frame has a width:height ratio of 1:1½, while an 8"x10" photo has a ratio of 1:1¼. Thus when a frame is blown up to become a borderless 8x10 it must be cropped on the top and/or bottom. In a portrait style photo the frame is not blown up as much, so it stays well within the 8x10 paper, leaving more margin on the sides than on top or bottom. If you see that uneven black line around the image, it means the photographer has used a *negative carrier* (a frame to hold the negative) slightly larger than the 35mm frame, and has printed the photo in its full frame, without cropping. If you look at old photos in art museums you will see the same line of the negative carrier around the image. This is a sign among photographers (or anyone else who understands what it means—like you, now) that the photographer framed the shot with his eye and his camera, rather than cropping it afterwards in the darkroom. While printing this way may be a point of pride for some photographers, it doesn't really matter a bit in the context of a P/R, and portrait style shots can also be created by enlarging and cropping the shot to the desired size and then having the printer drop a line in around the photo when it is reproduced, or by leaving the line out altogether. I've seen attractive photos created in all three manners. If your photographer does a portrait style photo for you he will pull back from you and keep a careful eye on the composition, framing the shot with his camera to avoid any extraneous objects in the photo.

You can see examples of these styles on Photo Page A: #1 and #2 are borderless headshots; #3 is the new portrait style, with a line dropped in by the printer, and #4 is the L.A. style. The choice of finish in all three styles is still matte or pearl rather than glossy. [By the way, you'll notice that all the photos in this book have a thin black line around the edge of the photo; this is to delineate between the photo and the page, and is not meant to be any kind of border.]

When I asked some people in the business about their preferences, I found wide acceptance of the more-than-head shots, whether L.A. style or portrait. Deborah Mendel, a talent agent in L.A., sees a definite trend toward outdoor pictures, with a natural look, not overly made up, and more honest. The question of headshot or as much as 3/4 body depends, she feels, on what is most flattering to the individual actor. Some actors are shown off best with full concentration on the face; others look better as a more complete figure, not simply a disembodied head. When I asked Michelle Ortlip, an independent Casting Director in New York, about her preference, she said she likes portrait shots because they give her a good sense of the person, including what his or her body looks like. Some actors go overboard, though, and she's seen a number of "kookie" photos that don't really work. Mark Ramont, Associate Artistic Director and head of casting at Circle Rep, likes portrait style too, and agreed with Michelle that it gives a better sense of the actor. Note that Michelle and Mark cast mainly for theatre; the headshot is still in demand for commercial and soaps because those casting people are interested in what the camera will see in close-up and because they want to be able to type actors quickly from headshots.

So now you're probably totally confused as to what style of photo to go for. If statistics are any help to you, at a recent open call in New York I counted 410 headshots, 39 portrait style (these all showed more than the head—some had a line around the photo, some didn't), 2 full body "L.A. type" shots, 3 composites, 1 color and 1 just plain weird (this was a headshot taken on a beach with other people sitting on the sand, out of focus, in the background). Photos received from a casting director ran about 10 portrait style to 40 headshots. That means that currently (Spring 1991) 80% - 90% of New York actors are still using borderless headshots. If you would like my personal prediction, I would say we're currently moving from the standard headshot into a larger range of acceptable photo styles: anything from head to full body, either borderless or with wide borders. I believe that for the next year or so there will be a strong trend toward the portrait style, and toward showing more of the arms and torso, but not necessarily full body. Right now, this look is interesting because it's new, and it stands out in a pile of headshots; if the trend continues, of course, and the ratio becomes 50% instead of 80-90%, the portrait style will cease to stand out so much. The only styles I would consider still "out" are glossy finishes and narrow (3/8") white borders. Otherwise, anything within the range we've been discussing is going to be acceptable.

If you are living in or moving to L.A., or if you work bicoastally, you will probably want to experiment with a photo showing more body, whether portrait style or borderless. If you're working in New York the choice of headshot or portrait style is up to you. But wherever you're working, it still makes sense to have at least one headshot as well, since many commercial and soap casting people still want to see one. As you go through the process of selecting photographers, discuss style with them, and ask about getting more than one style out of the shoot.

Theatre, Commercials, Soaps

In this book we will talk about three different *looks* you may want from your photos, for specific usage in three areas: theatre (which also includes film), commercial and soaps. These are still the norm, especially in New York, although I don't wish to overemphasize these three looks, as if some casting person were going to fix you with an icy glare and tell you "You're auditioning for a commercial, and this is your *soap* shot." Since you're going through this whole expensive process of getting photos made, you'll want to wind up with more than one photo. Whether you have two, three or four, in whatever style, and whether you label them theatre/commercial/soap or smiling/dramatic or even "Mom's favorite/boyfriend's favorite/my favorite" doesn't really matter. You'll send the photo that will be most effective in selling you for a particular job. What you should remember above all else is that the various *looks* you will achieve depend on what's going on in your head at the photo session, not just what you're wearing and whether the corners of your mouth turn up or down.

That being said, we'll start with some common misconceptions: theatre shots are more dramatic; commercial shots very upbeat; soap shots very sexy. My response to all three is "Yes, *but...*". Such generalizations have major pitfalls: theatre shots should not be grim and overly intense; commercial shots should not be superficial; soap shots should offer something more than pure sex—like *some* flicker of intelligence, perhaps.

When shooting a photo to be used for theatre and film, many actors tend to go very serious, with nary a hint of a smile, possibly in an attempt to project their depth as an actor. This strikes me as wrong-headed, since there's no way a photo really can project what kind of an actor you are. It *can*, however, say something about what kind of a person you are. Some people have big, smiling personalities, others do not. Going back to the idea of *including* the viewer or having a secret to share with him, you can see that this concept works equally well with or without a smile. A smile (though it need not be full out, all teeth in view) can work in your favor, just as one tends to be more drawn to a person with a great smile at first meeting. But in both cases, the picture and the person, it's what's going on *behind* the smile that really makes the meeting memorable. The risk in a "serious" shot is that it becomes closed and off-putting; what will prevent that is, again, a sense of *including* the viewer. In fact, don't fall into the trap of thinking in terms of smiling vs. serious. You want all your pictures to include and invite the viewer to share something with you. It is the subtext of *what you wish to share* that will make the picture happen. When you move from theatrical to commercial to soap shot, focus on how you are going to *vary the subtext*, not on whether or not you're going to smile.

One more caution about the theatrical shot in particular: to some actors (and to some photographers as well), "dramatic" means "dark" and the face is partially obscured in shadow. A theatrical photo needs to reveal your entire face with all features clearly defined; casting people don't want surprises to walk through the door. Have you ever watched a play in which the director and lighting designer were so concerned about "setting the mood" that you could hardly see the actors' faces? This might work for an isolated dramatic moment, but if it goes on all evening your eyes just get tired of working that hard, and you lose interest in the whole thing. Similarly, a highly shadowed photo can be striking on first glance, but when a director or casting person looks at it closely and can't really tell what your features are like, they are likely to pass you by rather than risk bringing you in.

In talking about commercial looks, we'll start with the traditional and work through some variations. The standard commercial headshot has always been the "P&G [Proctor & Gamble] Look": full front with a big smile, showing off one's gorgeous complexion, standard WASP features and as many perfect teeth as possible. Fortunately, Madison Avenue has lately begun to recognize the multi-ethnic and multi-generational realities of our population, and has even begun to inch past the "beautiful people only" theory of selling products. In an interview I did with commercial agent Anne Stein recently, she emphasized that the scope of people being used in commercials now really is much broader, with more ethnicity and "quirkiness" and therefore commercial casting people are looking favorably at more natural headshots.

The natural look, according to Stein, means to go easy on the hair, and perhaps experiment with a more casual pose, with a sweater or jacket, looking almost as though you've been caught off guard. She still recommended studio over outdoor shots, as studio lighting can be carefully controlled to assure the most flattering look. Also, since so many commercials are shot in studios, your headshot should show how you look in studio light. Regarding the old chestnut that you must show teeth in a commercial shot, so they know you've got good ones, Stein hesitated a bit. "You probably should have at least one shot with teeth," was her ultimate answer. "Of course, if your teeth are horrendous and you hide them, and you get in for an interview, they're still going to notice that you've got bad teeth, but at least you've gotten in. You do still have your P&G where they want the perfect midwestern mom, but you've also got your beer commercials, and the 'summer fun' commercials where people just aren't so perfect any more. Agents are going to make notes when you come in, 'nice hair, funny teeth,' but if it isn't a close-up shot, teeth won't matter that much."

I also interviewed Jean Rohn, Assistant Casting Director for *All My Children* to ask what she looked for in pictures. She too stressed the importance of having a photo that looks like the actor, saying "I must not be surprised when you walk in!" Women in particular, she felt, try to look too glamorous in a photo taken specifically for soaps, and overdo it on the airbrushing. "Retouching a photo to death takes off ten points; it doesn't behoove you to have a picture that doesn't represent you honestly."

Jean was not terribly concerned about a particular soap "look", feeling in fact that for the most part, two headshots were sufficient. She felt the one for commercials should be "a smile shot—they want to see your teeth," but that one other photo could service theatre, film and soaps. She did not have any particular preference for a headshot or fuller body shot, feeling it was up to the actor. But what she does look for, she said, is "something behind the eyes." In terms of clothing, again she did not feel an actor had to be terribly formal, and advised that women should not show cleavage. "We're looking at the face," she explained. "We have imaginations; I know people can change clothes!" Jewelry should be kept simple, with nothing to detract from the face, and hair should be off the face so the casting director can see the actor's face and eyes clearly. Also, she felt that the general preference among TV casting people is for a studio shot, because it's usually sharper than an outdoor shot. She remarked that some outdoor shots were too casual, although some can work, depending on what the actor is comfortable with and how he wants to sell himself.

Your decision to have two or three different photos made may be based largely on cost: if your photographer's package offers two and you don't want to go the extra expense for a third *and if you're happy with the two and feel they will cover all bases* then it's not necessary to go for a specific soap shot. Conversely, if you know you want three different looks, that may have an influence on your choice of photographer; you will lean toward those whose package offers three shots. If you're starting to feel confused, don't worry; in the next chapter you'll do some hard thinking about your own personal "look" as an actor. Once you've worked out for yourself where you're most castable, the decision as to how many shots you'll need should fall into place. If you were made to be the next torrid affair on *Guiding Light*, in the Chapter 4 we'll help you come up with a photo that proves it.

Names, Composites, Postcards

Whether you have your name printed on the front of your picture or not is a matter of personal taste as much as current style. The argument *for* the name is that every time a casting person looks at your picture, s/he is associating your name with it, and is more likely to remember you. Also, of course, should your picture ever become separated from your resume, there's no question about who's who. The argument *against* having your name on the picture is that then the casting person must turn it over to see who you are, and thus s/he will be more likely to read the resume on the back. There's also some subtle subtext going on—"you should *know* who this is." Generally, the L.A. shots described previously do not have the name on the front—presumably because L.A. is big on subtext, and/or because the printed name might conflict with the image created by the photo. In New York, however, many actors choose to print their name on their photo, whether they use a headshot or portrait style.

If you decide to print your name on the front of a headshot, you have three choices as to how to do it. You can print it in *knockout*, which means a white block is inserted on an appropriate place on the photo, and your name is printed in black inside that block. Or you can have it printed in *reverse*, with your name in white on a dark part of the photo; or you can simply have your name printed in black type on a light part of the photo. In a portrait style photo, the name usually is printed in black type in the white border, although I have also seen the name printed in an appropriate place on the photo image, in black or reverse. Examples of these techniques can be seen on photos #1, #2 and #3; we didn't bother to print names on the rest of the photos because they're illustrating various technical points. If you decide *not* to have your name imposed on your photo, I strongly suggest you write or stamp it on the reverse side of the photo. That way if the photo and resume should ever become separated, there will be no confusion about who you are. You can have a rubber stamp made up, with your name and contact phone number, and stamp the back of your pictures when you get the copies made up. It's best to stamp on the back of a dark area in the photo, to eliminate any chance of the ink showing through.

A *composite* is a sheet that is favored over a headshot by some commercial agents for their clients. On one side it usually has a single 8x10 headshot with the actor's name and perhaps phone number; on the back are four or five smaller photos along with a few vital statistics, but no resume. The smaller pictures put the actor in commercial type situations: sitting on the hood of a car; mopping a floor; holding a product; sitting at a typewriter. They will show the actor in a variety of clothing, from executive to casual, perhaps with and without glasses, more and less glamorous, but all definitely showing "commercial types." I have also seen composites that are printed on 17"x11" paper, folded in half to 8 1/2"x11". Pictures are printed on the front and back, and inside the front sheet and a full resume is printed inside the back sheet. A variety of papers are used, much lighter than the photographic paper used for headshots, usually either coated (glossy) or textured.

Composites are expensive ventures which should not be embarked upon unless and until you have a commercial agent who believes s/he can market you most effectively with a composite. If your agent feels that strongly about using a composite, you can bet s/he will feel just as strongly about how it should look—the number of pictures, poses, clothing, paper and everything else that's involved. All the material in this book regarding the photo shoot applies equally to composites, with the logical adjustments for creating different character types, so once you've read this you will have the resources to come up with an excellent composite. However, we strongly advise that you *don't try to do a composite before you have a commercial agent*, and then only if the agency strongly prefers composites over single shots. There's no point in spending that kind of money first, then finding an agent who prefers to use headshots or wants you to have a composite but doesn't like the pictures you have.

Postcards, on the other hand, are something you definitely should do on your own, at the same time you do your P/R. A postcard is just what it sounds like—a picture postcard, only of *you* instead of the Grand Canyon. You will use it after you've sent out your P/R's to casting directors and agents, as a periodic follow-up to keep your face in their minds. It's much cheaper than sending P/R's and doesn't clutter their files, which they appreciate. Most of the services that reproduce theatrical photos do postcards also, frequently at a special package rate. You can choose the one photo you think is best for general use, or have a second set made with a different shot. Some actors put two headshots side by side on a postcard. If this is your choice, then the two photos are very different—for instance, with and without glasses. It's your choice, and represents a relatively economic way of getting your face out there, so don't scrimp on postcards. Whether you have your name on the front of your 8x10 or not, you definitely want it printed on your postcard, along with your service number.

Dealing with Photographers When You Live Outside the Center(s) of the Universe

If you don't live in NYC or L.A., but do live in a city which has an active professional theatre community (Chicago, Boston, Atlanta, Seattle, San Francisco, etc.), you should be able to choose from several professional photographers who are experienced in theatrical photography. However, you may be in a situation where you don't have direct access to such photographers; for instance, you're going to college in a relatively small city with a limited selection of photographers, none of whom have much experience with theatrical photos. What to do?

First of all, consider when and why you need the photos. If you are about to graduate and plan an immediate move to a major theatre city, you should wait until you get there to have your photos done. Sure, it would be nice to hit town with your P/R's all ready to go, but it's not worth a major expense at an out-of-town photographer's if there's a chance you're going to make the move and immediately decide your headshot is all wrong for the city you're in. If your headshot looks unprofessional compared to the norm when you hit NYC or L.A., you've wasted your money. Smaller cities have their own theatre communities, and they may have their own subtle variations on the look of a P/R—frequently due to the influence of the one or two photographers who do the bulk of the theatrical work. Better to arrive in town and focus immediately on getting a professional P/R done there, with the local "look" which marks you as a part of that specific theatrical community, than to announce that you're an outsider every time you show your picture. Some of these theatre communities can be very tight, and you want your P/R to make it easier, not harder, for you to break in.

On the other hand, suppose you've still got a couple years of school left, but you're looking for summer stock work; or you're a senior looking towards graduate schools and professional internships. In these cases you need a good, professional looking P/R to send out, but you may not have access to experienced theatrical photographers. You can get a good headshot from a studio photographer who doesn't have experience with theatrical photos, as long as you are very well prepared before you go into the shoot.

First, read and understand all the points in this book, even before you start looking at photographers. Being clear on precisely what you need will compensate for the photographer's inexperience with the theatrical style. Secondly, as you meet with photographers, remember it is crucial that you find one who is open to the idea of altering his or her normal studio style just a bit, to fit your needs. Bring this book along, and use our photos as a frame of reference for the photographer, so he or she knows exactly the look you need. If one seems resistant to making any adjustments, find another photographer. Finally, prepare very carefully so that you are confident you've made the right choices regarding clothes, hair and makeup and any changes for different shots, and that you can "direct yourself" during the shoot, as we'll discuss in Chapter 4. If your photographer is not used to working with actor clients, then you'll have to compensate with your own preparation.

Chapter 3

Organize *Now* to Get a Picture that Works for You

If you're the kind of actor who never feels quite as organized as you think you ought to be, here's a good place to start. Getting a Picture/Resume done (or redone) can be either a painful experience drawn out over several months and fraught with anxiety which undermines your self-confidence, or it can be a well-planned, promptly executed piece of business that leaves you feeling upbeat, confident and eager to spread your "new" face around the business. To help you get in gear, look in the Appendix at Worksheet #1, the Planning Schedule. It's a very simple form, designed to help you start thinking about your P/R as a specific goal which you will reach within a reasonable amount of time. We suggest aiming for 1-2 weeks for you to do your research, another 1-2 weeks for the actual photo session, and one more week for the final results. Depending on how quickly your chosen photographer can schedule you, you could have a gorgeous new P/R ready to go within a month of buying this book. So look ahead at your life a little, and set a reasonable time-frame (don't try to get your picture done the week you're opening a show, or two days before you're flying home for the holidays), then make your P/R a top priority, and don't take on less important commitments that might endanger your schedule. Set up your schedule on the planning sheet, and stick to it.

Researching Photographers

You're going to get the names of photographers from two sources: fellow actors and photographers' advertisements. It's always nice to get a personal reference on a photographer, because not only can you see the product, but you can also ask about the shooting session and the photographer's way of working. Having filled out your planning schedule and set aside a period for research, dive right into it. Don't wait for chance meetings with other actors; make phone calls to those whom you remember as having good photos, and arrange a meeting to look at their headshots (and look at their contact sheets too, if you can).

Even if you have a reasonably long list of photographers recommended by friends, you should look in the trade papers for theatrical photographers' ads. If you're having your photo done in New York, *Back Stage* always has photographers' ads in the back; similarly, *Drama Logue* in L.A., *Audition News* in Chicago, *New England Entertainment Digest* in Boston, *Call Board* in San Francisco, etc. Look at the ads of the photographers who have been recommended to you, and compare them to other ads. Many ads will list prices, so you can do some comparative shopping even before you start contacting photographers. Many cities have their own actors' guidebook: *The New York Casting & Survival Guide*; L.A.'s *Working Actor's Guide*; *The Source* in Boston and *The Actor's Handbook* in Seattle, all run ads and lists of theatrical photographers (see Appendix for all these sources). Other sources to check are bulletin boards in drama book shops, Equity offices, or any actors' resource organization you may have access to in your city. You can also look in the yellow pages, but be sure a listing specifies theatrical photos, or call and ask if they do theatrical headshots.

From the list of the ten or so most likely prospects that you made on your planning sheet, you probably want to follow through on about six. If you're in a small city, you might have a more limited number of photographers to choose from, and you may only visit four; on the other hand, if you're getting a little obsessive about this by now, you may visit eight or ten. It's probably better to expend the extra energy and see more than to wonder if you've made the right choice. However, in most cases after seeing six photographers you'll probably have found the one you want to work with. *We strongly suggest that you read chapters 1-4 thoroughly and look through the photos carefully, before you even start calling photographers.* Once you're familiar with all the terminology, and clear about exactly what you want, make extra copies of Worksheet #2 - Photographer Comparison, so that you have one for each photographer you're going to call and/or visit.

Begin by calling each photographer to introduce yourself and explain the style of photo you're thinking about: studio or outdoor, headshot and/or fuller body. Ask if they have a style preference, and which style(s) they shoot most often. Then ask a few of the questions on your list, such as their fee (which may eliminate some of them right away if you are on a tight budget). If you like the sound of the photographer on the phone, set up a time to drop by his or her studio for a "look-see," at which you will have the rest of your questions answered and look through a portfolio. If you hang up the phone with a negative feeling after any of these calls, drop that photographer from your list and pick another. There should be no fee and no obligation for the look-see; it's standard procedure for an actor to ask when he or she can "come by and look at your book" (portfolio), and if a photographer implies on the phone or in person that you've made any kind of commitment by simply looking, walk away.

Many actors, especially those new to the business, are intimidated by the process of selecting a photographer, and allow the photographer to control the entire situation. Work against that impulse, because what you're looking for is a true collaboration. Trust your instincts; "audition" the photographer on the phone and at the look-see. If someone makes you feel he's doing you a favor to even consider shooting your photos, pass him by; you're shopping for a service and *you* determine whose service you like best. It doesn't matter a whit if he's 'the best in the business'; if you're trembling in front of the camera your shots will look terrible. I can't stress this enough: remember that *if anything about the process intimidates you, it will inhibit your ability to show your real self in the photo session.*

These are the questions you'll want to ask the photographer, all of which you'll find on Worksheet #2:

- Exactly what is included in the shooting fee?
- How many rolls of film will you shoot?
- How many finished prints are included?
- Who owns the negative?
- Will you provide or arrange for a hair & make-up artist? What will it cost?

- How many changes do you allow? Does your stylist alter hair and make-up for change of clothing?

- How long will the session last? Will you be working with me alone? *(sometimes larger studios are set up so a photographer is doing two shoots at a time, with the help of assistants)*

- How soon can I see the proof sheets? How soon can I have the final prints?

- What kind of guarantee do you offer? Is there an extra charge for reshooting if needed?

- How much do you charge for extra prints?

- Will you provide or arrange for retouching? What will it cost?

- Do you make your own reproduction prints? If not, do you recommend someone?

- How far in advance do I have to book? Do you require a deposit? Is there a cancellation fee?

- Do you offer a discount if I return for updated photos?

If some of these terms, like *retouching* or *reproduction prints* are unfamiliar, don't worry, they will be explained in the next chapter. Remember, *read all the chapters on photos (1 – 4)* before you start making calls.

By contacting at least six different photographers, a pattern will emerge, and you'll discover the "standard deal" for your particular city. There probably won't be a huge variation among photographers, since one would expect them all to keep abreast of the market and know what the competition is offering. You will have your own budget restrictions, of course, but it's generally best to consider photographers in the middle price range. One might do well to be suspicious of any deal that sounds too good to be true, because it probably is. All good photographers have legitimate costs, and can only do so many jobs if they are to give full attention to each one. A very low price tag may indicate a rush job, or inferior quality. On the other hand, paying a very high price for a photographer is something like buying designer clothes; you may be paying more for the "imprint" than the actual quality. A photographer who gets top dollar for his reputation may be called the best in the business, but he also may be more concerned with his "signature" than with giving you what will serve you best.

Looking at the Book

When you look through the photographer's book, remember that you're searching for a photographer who can capture the *essence* of a subject. Do his pictures look alive and active and interesting, or posed? Are there thoughts going through the minds of these people, or are they simply pretty? Do the prints of these people look real or are they technically manipulated to look glamorous? Here are some specific points to look for in a portfolio (these too are included in Worksheet #2):

- Skin tones (skin texture) should be real, not airbrushed or retouched.

- Lighting and contrast should separate the face and hair from the background color. Blonde hair should look blonde, not unnaturally light or dark; dark hair should not blend into background.

- Notice the cropping: in a standard headshot, the eyes should be close to the picture's center and the head should be more than 1/2 the picture size.

- Neither clothing nor background (especially on outdoor shots) should pull focus away from the actor.

- Lighting should be even, soft; like a slightly overcast day, or light through a skylight.

- There should be no sharp shadow lines; no places on the face should be in such dark shadow as to obscure features.

- Make sure the pictures don't have a pronounced *grain* or texture to them (see Glossary).

- Subject's focus should be with eyes into the camera.

- Are the eyes working? The eyes are the most important element, whether in a headshot or portrait style. Don't get caught up in cosmetics; the fact that every hair is in place won't get an actor an audition, the life in the eyes will.

- The people in the photos should look different from each other. They should reflect the actors' different personalities, rather than the photographer's particular style. A photographer's "signature" doesn't get you the audition.

- Trust your impressions of the book. Do you feel you know something about the actors in the photos? Do they look as though they're in the same room as you? In the same *world* as you?

Looking through the photos we've included, particularly #13 – 24, will help you recognize technical problems in a photographer's portfolio. Here are some other, less technical tips from Tom about selecting a photographer:

- Find someone you can feel comfortable with at the shoot; if the photo is to capture your essence, there needs to be a certain quality of abandon at the session.

- Likewise, find a photographer who will take care of all the physical necessities at the session, so you can be capricious.

- A cosmetically perfect, controlled picture won't necessarily look like you, because it won't necessarily reflect your own personality.

- After you look at all the books, leave it alone for a while. The right person will become evident to you—whoever *feels* best to you is the photographer to use.

Your Different "Looks"

While you're researching photographers, start doing some research on yourself, too. Assuming that you are going for all three looks—theatrical, commercial and soap—then you need to think about yourself in the context of each, and choose make-up and clothing accordingly. Remember to be true to who you are, rather than going for the look that you think a casting person wants to see, because unless the look is right for you, the photo will be stilted. Also remember that although we will be talking about these three looks, you shouldn't over-emphasize the differences; they should all be *you*, and you may frequently send out your "commercial" shot for a particular theatre audition, or your "legit" shot for an industrial, etc., depending on the role.

It sounds obvious, but you must also remember that you need to be able to look like your picture when you walk in for an audition. If your soap shot is so glamorous that you would have to have your hair done before going to an audition, you're working against yourself. When you think about your look for each shot, think in terms of what you generally do (or what you feasibly *could* do) to get ready for an audition for theatre, a commercial, or a soap. A general rule of thumb is that your legit shot is your natural self, in the most positive sense—when you're rested, relaxed, in a positive frame of mind, rarin' to go. Your commercial look is a little more styled and polished, or upscale and professional, depending on whether you might be considered the All-American or the Executive Type. In your soap shot you're going to show the more seductive, sultry side of you.

As you start preparing for your photo session, take some time for a little objective self-examination. Think about your physical characteristics and the inner qualities you want to bring out. As an exercise, write down the qualities you feel you possess, and think about whether your clothes match them. Which of your qualities predominate your acting? How can you support these in the clothing you choose for your photo? This is a time for a realistic but positive appraisal of your qualities, inside and out. There's no point in wishing that your eyes were set wider apart, or that your earlobes were smaller. Work with what you have and choose clothes and make-up to emphasize the best of you and subtly downplay whatever you're not so happy with. Some frank input from a very few *trusted* people in the business could be useful at this point, if there's a casting person or director you feel you can go to with your old P/R in hand for some candid opinions.

It is also helpful to do some research into "types" at this point. Since I've already thrown around the terms *look* and *style*, I should explain how I distinguish *type* from those terms: *type* is a general category used by casting people to communicate how a particular actor would normally be cast, or what kind of actor is needed for a given role. Traditional theatrical types are: juvenile; ingenue; character man/woman; heavy; leading man; leading lady. More contemporary types used in commercial and film might be: executive; family man; young mom; hooker; all-American; street kid, etc. The concept of type is anathema to most actors, who desire wholeheartedly to believe that a good actor can play *any* character. Maybe in actor heaven you'll find a short balding Romeo and a 180-pound Juliet, but please be realistic when you're spending a lot of money on a P/R, and accept the fact that not only does type-casting still exist, it still predominates. Watch commercials carefully for a few days, and sort the people you see into categories, then try to determine where you fit in. Don't think, "*I could do* that commercial spot" but rather, "*would they cast me* in that commercial spot?" Do you look like the young mom, the gorgeous model, the hip dude, or the beer-drinking yuppie? Follow the same routine with soaps, and if you are *not* the love-interest type, consider how you might realistically be used: consulting doctor, assistant D.A., etc.

This book is not meant to be a treatise on casting for film and TV, nor on how to get your career going, beyond the putting together of a P/R that will work for you. But in order to do that, you must begin with a realistic assessment of where you fit into the entertainment industry as it exists today. In my discussion with Anne Stein, while she indicated that commercial casting is getting a little more realistic and stretching the P&G look to fit a wider variety of real people, she still emphasized that there are many good actors who will continue to find it hard to do commercials, because their type does not fit the Madison Avenue concept of who's buying what product.

If you're not working within the framework of reality as far as casting goes, the result can be a P/R that works against your type (for instance, a photo that over-glamorizes you), which will be completely counter-productive. Your P/R will set up expectations in the casting person's mind that you can't fulfill when you walk in the door. Far better to accept that there are some types you will never play (or at least, not until you have your own production company), stop pursuing those dreams, and find where your true strengths lie within the casting game.

Clothing

Does it sound sexist to suggest that women are more aware than men of which styles, cuts and colors are most flattering to them? It can't be helped, we're deluged with it; you can't pick up a women's magazine that doesn't have at least one article on how to determine which hem length, haircut or makeup shade works best with your body, face or coloring. But man or woman, if this is an area you're not overly comfortable with, get some help in the form of outside opinions. Have a friend over to help you rummage through the closet when you pick out clothing for your photos. As you do, remember that in a black and white photo you're dealing with *contrast*, not with color, since different colors will show up as various shades of gray.

An advantage of sticking with the traditional headshot is that you only have to worry about your collar line; the more body shown in the photo, the more clothing you have to pick out! Many portrait style photos show the full torso, in which case layers work well: an open-necked shirt with a vest; a leotard with a blouse over it; a shirt and a jean jacket, etc. These break up the torso, so your face isn't competing with one large mass of clothing. It is possible to get a similar effect with a shirt alone, if it has a nice texture or is loosly fitting and worn open-necked with the sleeves pushed up. Although most women will wear a skirt to an audition, slacks or stylish jeans can work well in a casually posed photo; if the legs are seen at all in the frame of the photo, they're rarely emphasized.

Photos 9 – 12 show some examples of common mistakes actors can make with clothing and make-up. There are a few general rules which will help avoid these:

- Stay away from both white and black, as they wreak havoc with lighting and contrast.

- A v-neckline lengthens the neck, while a round neckline shortens it; a v-neck shirt with collar generally frames the face pleasingly.

- Turtlenecks hide the neck completely, and generally should be avoided.

- Avoid bold patterns, though subdued plaids and stripes can work.

- Also avoid jewelry, which can shine and distract. Women with pierced ears should generally stick to a small hoop or simple stud earrings instead of large, dangling ones.

- If you use glasses in a photo, they should be frames only, without lenses.

- Try to wear something that makes you *feel* as good as you look. A favorite shirt that has some pleasant associations or history behind it can help you relax at the photo session.

If you generally wear glasses, should you wear them in your photo? It really depends on how much a part of your everyday appearance they are. If you don't wear contacts and generally wear glasses to your auditions, it's sensible to show them in at least one photo. If you generally act without glasses, however, don't use them in your photo, except as a character prop. Glasses can be very useful in that regard, because they can change your appearance remarkably, while being less risky than funny hats or other props. So if you think you have a marketable look in glasses, by all means use them in one of your photos, even if you have 20-20 vision.

When you go to your shooting session, you'll take along changes of clothing for your various looks. For your theatre/film shot, pick clothing to support the introspective, thoughtful side of yourself. You might choose dark colors, open collars, garments that you are especially fond of in terms of color, texture and history. Denim or leather jackets can work well, or sweaters, without jewelry or props. You want to feel confident, relaxed and ready to work.

In thinking about your commercial shot, consider whether you fit more into the "all-American" (be it young mom or outdoorsy beer-drinker) or the "upscale" business executive type. If the first, choose casual clothes in light colors with open collars. Patterns are acceptable if not too contrasty; stay away from white. Sweater and shirt combinations are good for both men and women; a subdued plaid, open-necked shirt with a sweater over it is a popular choice. You want clothing that supports an outgoing, enthusiastic smile, and you should avoid jewelry, hats or props. If you're going for the upscale look, you'll want business clothing such as a blazer or jacket with tie or a bow blouse, with very conservative jewelry (i.e., watch, wedding ring). You might use glasses (without lenses), but no other props.

For a soap shot, women can go with something more glamorous, with a lower neckline (make up all skin evenly), but use caution and taste in picking these clothes. It's very important in this shot for a woman to assess exactly where her type lies. A blatantly suggestive neckline, for instance, will undermine your credibility, and yet if you have the potential for a "hot" role, you want the casting director to see it. Find something that you think shows your potential, but that you wouldn't feel ridiculous wearing to an audition. Hair and make-up can emphasize the classy, glamorous aspect. If you're a man and a romantic lead possibility, don't go with a suit and tie, but you don't have to get too trendy either. Shirt open to the waist with gold chains entangled in hairy chest is definitely out; actually, the same clothing you choose for your theatre/film shot will probably work, with a change of expression as we'll discuss later.

Some photographers keep a few all-purpose articles of clothing on hand in their studio, and may suggest you use them instead of or in addition to whatever you've brought to the shoot. Generally these are shirts or jackets that they've found work very well in black and white photos, in terms of hue and intensity and neckline. In fact, there's one plaid shirt used by a NYC photographer that's probably found its way onto dozens of actors and actresses, being unisex as well as all-purpose. If the photographer is persistent about a certain shirt, let him do some shots in it, since you never can tell what you'll discover on the contact sheet. But if you've chosen your clothes carefully, with an eye toward what works well in black and white and is most flattering to you, you shouldn't need to substitute. And remember, clothes in which you feel good will make you more relaxed and positive at the shoot.

Women — Hair and Make-up

A woman definitely should wear some make-up for the photo session, even if she normally wears little or no make-up and considers herself the "natural" type. A good translucent base evens out skin tones; the camera sees shades and gradations that the human eye doesn't, and these need to be evened out. Since eyes tend to flatten out in the studio, make-up is needed to sharpen the lines and add depth. On the other hand, even if you normally wear a considerable amount of make-up, you don't want to hide behind make-up in your photo; you're trying to bring out your real self, not disguise it. As with clothing, the amount and type of make-up also varies with the purpose of the headshot (theatre/film, commercial, soap). If you're trying to get those three different looks out of your session, you will want to change hair and make-up accordingly, along with the clothing changes.

The most important thing about the make-up for your theatre/film picture is that it be consistent with the way you will look when you go to an audition. If you tend to wear little street make-up, try to use no more than normal in the photo session, so you can keep it consistent in your daily audition rounds. Your commercial make-up might be slightly more styled or upscale, while your soap shot would be more glamorous. Hair follows accordingly, and you should take these changes into account when you decide which sequence to use in shooting, so the hair and make-up changes can be done most efficiently; generally you'll start with the simplest and add glamour as you go on.

A big question for an actress in preparing for her photo session is whether to do her own hair and make-up or to use a professional make-up artist. Although a professional adds considerably to the cost of the photos, if you end up with a photo that doesn't work for you because of your hair and make-up, then you've wasted all the money and effort you put into the whole process. Also, if you have qualms about your ability to do a good job on your own, it's better to go with a professional, because eliminating the *worry* about having the right hair and make-up will make you more relaxed and natural at the shoot.

Expect to pay between $75 - 150 for a professional to do your hair and make-up, with changes during the shoot as discussed. Most photographers will supply a hair and make-up artist on request, or will recommend one or more people you can contact. However, a photographer should not insist that you use his make-up person as a condition of the shooting session. Clarify each photographer's policy when you call or visit their studio, and get the name of the make-up artist. This is another area for research when you're looking at fellow actors' P/R's; ask about the make-up person as well as about the photographer. As with the photographer, you want to feel comfortable with the make-up artist, so that s/he is bringing out *your* look, not creating a look s/he thinks you should fit into.

This last point is probably the best argument (even stronger than the money factor) for doing your own hair and make-up, *if you really have confidence in your abilities in this area*. Before deciding whether to do your own make-up and hair, you might want to try a practice session, and have a friend take some black and white polaroid shots to study the effect. If you are pleased with the results and believe that you can do the best job of presenting yourself, then by all means, go for it.

If you have decided to do your own hair and make-up, here are some points to keep in mind:

- Use a good quality base that covers without caking the skin, so your natural skin tones show.

- Don't attempt to cover attractive skin features, like freckles.

- It's essential to remember that you are making up for black and white film, so that you will be concerned with shadow and highlight, not color. Any color you apply which is darker than your skin tone will shadow, or deepen that area, while a lighter color will highlight a feature and make it more prominent.

- This means cheek color should go lower to accent the cheekbone; if it is applied on the cheekbone (as you would in your normal daytime make-up, to add color) it will take out the contour.

- Eyeshadow works the same way; it will not read as color, but will deepen your eye sockets.

- Lipstick is another example of color being meaningless—it is the contrast to your skin, not the color, that will show.

- Eyeliner should be soft, applied with a brush sparingly, with very little on the lower lid.

- Use mascara as you would use it normally.

- If you have long, straight hair, you need enough of a set to give it some fullness and body on the sides so that it frames your face attractively.

- The day before you have your photo taken is *not* the time to try out a new perm! Give a new "do" at least a week to be sure you know how to handle it.

Men — Hair and Make-up

Men have things easier than women in the hair and make-up department, and generally will take care of their own needs. When you make your appointment, find out if the photographer has make-up you can use to cover blemishes or your beard. Most of them do, but if not, bring your own translucent powder and/or base. Men shouldn't be made up too much, Tom explained, because while women want an even skin texture, men don't; part of a man's attractiveness in his photo is the history in his face, and too much make-up tends to obscure that. (Don't you love that? Women get older, men get history.) Usually all that's necessary is a very light coat of powder, although if you have a very heavy beard you might want to use a little bit of cream base to lighten it, as photos tend to accent dark beards.

Speaking of beards, a beard or mustache can alter an actor's look so much that it is very convenient to have pictures available as illustrations. Often an actor who has grown a beard for a current role will come into an audition with a bare-faced photo to show the director, and with good reason, since a beard can add several years onto an actor's apparent age. If you are an actor who frequently wears a beard, you might want to get the most out of a photo session by doing a full range of facial hair—first shooting with full beard and mustache, then shaving to mustache only, then clean-shaven. Shave carefully, and if you have had a beard for a long time be prepared to add make-up so there's no abrupt line. Men who don't normally wear a beard might want to try the first part of the session with the "Don Johnson" look of a few days' growth, and then shave for the remainder.

Men should begin to think about their hair style as soon as they decide to have a new picture done. Avoid a haircut that is so trendy as to type you out of general categories; i.e., shaved sides and spikes are going to take you out of the young doctor heartthrob category to a soap casting director. Very long hair can be detrimental also: since the actor is a professional, one would assume he would cut his hair if required, but if it obviously has been growing for quite a while, a director might pass on the actor rather than require him to get a haircut. If an actor uses a hairpiece he should definitely have photos with and without. As with beards, the difference in an actor's appearance with more and less hair can be startling, and a director should be shown the possibilities. Finally, allow at least a few days after a new haircut to schedule your photo session to avoid that slightly unnatural, freshly cut look.

Chapter 4

At the Studio

"So many actors tell me that they're not photogenic," Tom says, "as if they're sure there's some mysterious skill to having their photo taken, and they're no good at it. It's the *photographer's* job to have the skill; the actor's job is just to drop her guard. The only *skill* is the same one you use constantly as an actor." That fear of not being "photogenic" is the single greatest impediment to an actor at a photo session, Tom explained, and he became almost irate (for Tom) as he talked about photographers who intimidate actors. "You're not doing this for the approval of the photographer. Yet some photographers will take a very strong stand on how things should be, and actors will be *quaking* in front of them. That's not how to get a good picture." We'll try now to explain how *you* can control the photo session, to be sure that you will get a good picture.

By now you've gone through some painstaking research and come up with the best photographer for you, and you've put an equal amount of time and effort into thinking about your "looks" for the session, selecting clothing and considering hair and make-up. In your final preparations for your shoot, set the time for the session in accordance with the time of day you look the best and feel the most active. Try to get a full night's sleep for *several days running* before the shoot. Lack of sleep can play havoc with your eyes, but so can trying to catch up on sleep over just one night. Treat yourself kindly the day before, and approach the session with a positive frame of mind. You should bring along some of your favorite music, remembering that you want to be alive and "up", not simply relaxed. To show your inner life, you want to be neither overly mellow nor too tense. And don't make the mistake of "relaxing" with any alcohol or drugs; even one glass of wine will instantly dull the eyes. From your previous contacts with your photographer, on the phone and at the look-see, you have concluded that you can establish a rapport with him/her, and that you have confidence in his/her work. From the moment you arrive at the studio, try to relax with your hair and make-up person and enjoy the process.

Since a photographer's studio is foreign territory for many people, we've included photo #23 to give you an indication of what to expect. The background material will go to various shades of gray, depending on how it is lit. Backgrounds which have some texture—vague swirls and such—are increasing in popularity with the rise of the portrait style shot, in which more background is visible. The lighting for your session should be diffuse and reflected, not direct, as direct light produces harsh shadows. There should always be something between the subject (you) and the source of light, be it an umbrella, a flat reflector, a box, etc. The best lighting angle, as you might remember from your stagecraft class, is 45° from above and from the side. This gives the most natural shadows and highlights on your face. Since you've found a photographer you can trust, one assumes that everything you see in the studio will reinforce your confidence. If anything seems questionable, however, ask for a mirror. If you see any sharp shadows, show them to the photographer, and ask for the light to be more diffused.

When you look at your eyes, most often you will see the reflections of two lights, one distinct, above, and one softer and curved, below (this from a reflector which fills in shadows under eyes, jowls and chin). More than two lights reflected in your eyes can give a strange look to the photo, and fewer can mean loss of sparkle, so ask the photographer about either situation. However, some photographers get good results from lights positioned at four "corners" around the camera, and any extra reflections in your eyes can be touched out. You should feel comfortable asking your photographer technical questions like these, and it makes sense to calm any worries before the session starts. However, you don't want to project a belligerent attitude or sound as though you mistrust his/her capabilities. Any professional can get hostile fairly quickly if that happens. You have already chosen a photographer whose portfolio you felt was excellent, and if those pictures looked good, yours should too.

Outdoor lighting should have the same softness as that which is achieved in the studio with reflectors. Photos should not be shot in bright sun, which causes harsh shadows. On the other hand, shooting even in light shade means using faster film, so the photo can end up grainy. For these reasons an overcast day is best, so if you're doing an outdoor session, you and your photographer will need to schedule according to the weather.

Background is an important part of planning the outdoor shot. Most photographers probably have scouted a favorite outdoor background near their studio, and this is something you should ask about at the look-see if you know you want outdoor shots. If s/he has no suggestions, then you'll have to scout around yourself. Look for a background that is not too light, and that doesn't have too much contrast or "rhythm" like bricks or architectural elements. For example, the side of a darkish stucco building is more suitable than either a very light concrete block building or a brick one. Parks with greenery that can be thrown out of focus offer good texture and probably the right shade of gray for a background. Avoid extraneous objects in the background. Also, find someplace where you will feel comfortable. If it's too exposed to the public view, you may feel uneasy and distracted. If you frequent a particular place in a park that offers some seclusion and that isn't too far from the photographer, that could be an ideal background.

Acting Yourself for the Camera

Now that you and your photographer are all ready to go, the crucial element remains: how are you going to help the camera capture that irresistible inner you who is going to leap off the page at casting directors? The key is what is going on *within* you while the photographer is shooting, the *subtext* that the camera will reveal, beyond the perfect hair and make-up and open collared jean jacket.

Some photographers are wonderful at bringing this out during the session, and others aren't. Tom is great at it because he is a director and an actor himself. Since that's a combination you probably won't find in many photographers, we'll talk about how you can do for yourself what I've seen Tom do for an actor right at the shoot. You can prepare yourself for your photo session the way you would for an audition or an acting class, so if your photographer is not helping you get the subtext you can do it on your own.

In a photo, *passive* translates as dull, moody or lethargic. In order to make your headshot natural and exciting you want to create *a moment captured in active time*, not a passive pose, and in order to do this you must have action on your mind. If you're thinking about yourself or what you look like, you're not allowing yourself to be in the moment. *Adjectives freeze, verbs free.* This concept is the same one you use in your acting work; it's the difference between trying to play an emotion and playing an *action* or *intention*. When doing a scene you're not trying "to be angry." Instead you're trying "to hurt him back" or "to make her stop"—you choose for your character simple *actions* in order to get what you want, and the *emotion* occurs as a result. Similarly, in a photo session, instead of trying to "look happy" you should be thinking something like "Come here! I really want to show you _____!" Fill in the blank with something that elicits a happy response, one so positive that you can't wait to share it.

Sharing is the key. Tom's premise is that if the actor can learn to truly *include* the camera, the result will be a vital photo. The photo reaches out and grabs the viewer, because it is inviting the viewer to come into the world of the actor, implying that there's something very special there to share. In your theatrical or soap shot there is an added *subtext* to the invitation, some very special mystery or secret that the actor has and is letting us in on. In a commercial shot, you can drop the subtext and simply open up the invitation to something fun and upbeat.

In order to truly share with the camera, it is crucial to endow the camera with the being of *a particular person from your own experience*; if your choice is a specific person who is important to you, it will automatically bring life to your eyes. The eye of the camera must become a dear friend, a loved one, someone exciting that you're trying to get involved with—a specific individual who sets off an upbeat, excited response in you. You may use different people for different reactions, but you need to have some ideas about subtext in your head before you get to the shoot. What images will you use, what wonderful plan do you have, who is the special person you're inviting to join in with you? Write your ideas down on your Planning Schedule. This is part of your checklist, as vital as the clothing you'll bring and the make-up you'll use for each shot. Following are some ideas that can help plan how you will come to life at the photo session.

Your theatre/film shot can be somewhat thoughtful and have the most mystery to it, but keep it active. Think of planning, or hatching something, and of coiled energy—something is about to happen. Try hatching a bright, positive plan that you can approach with enthusiasm. If it doesn't elicit an actual smile, find at least a twinkle somewhere; avoid a brooding "Chekovian" subtext, which will tend to read overly dramatic or pretentious. You can afford to show your own particular brand of mystery, whether that is in the impish or Rambo vein. Think "Come here, I want to tell you about my plan."

In commercial shots as we said, you can drop the subtext. You want an active, natural smile that is integrated—your eyes must smile, as well as your mouth. You want to show your teeth without featuring them, and avoid that wooden toothy grin. Again the emphasis is on the *invitation*, and a good tool here is to use a child you know well as your object, the person you're inviting. Call the child to come to you so you can show her something very special. The commercial shot is one you want to be enthusiastic and very open, so the idea of sharing with a child can help you to keep it simple and real. Say a sentence out loud: an enthusiastic "come with me!" can help present a bright expression, and the word "me" shows teeth. This works very well for the "young mom" image, or the All-American type. If you're more the upscale executive type you want a similar enthusiasm, but at a more adult level, where the stakes are a little higher. Choose your subject accordingly: a client, a co-worker, someone you're delighted to be helping out with something they need. Again, use a specific person, someone you know, for all these images.

For the soap shot, carry this idea into something more provocative so that there's a sexy, playful secret in your eyes. Tom uses the idea "come here" when coaching his clients, but explains the differences this way: "In commercials it's 'come here to play,' in theatre it's 'come here to plan,' and in soaps it's 'come here to...' In a soap shot you should envision a particularly juicy sexy love object and *with your eyes alone* draw it to you." Play around with some ideas ahead of time, and write down the ones that seem to work best for you. You want to be fresh and spontaneous, so don't over-prepare (there's no need to memorize a sequence of actions, for instance), but do enough preparation so you're not under pressure to come up with brilliant ideas on the spot.

If you are going for a shot showing full or partial body, it is obviously very important that your eyes are "working". Although your eyes will be proportionally smaller and hence somewhat less significant than in a full headshot, they still carry much of the impact of the picture. Use the same acting techniques we've just described, being sure to follow through with your body. Keep your face and eyes active, and let that same energy flow through your body, just as you do when performing. You can help yourself by avoiding a completely relaxed physical position that pulls your energy down: a sense of leaning *toward* the camera will include, while leaning *away* will distance the viewer. Be conscious too, of the "body language" of the position. Your physical attitude, the way you stand, sit or lean, can convey sexuality, excitement, arrogance, any number of attributes. Be sure your body is not in conflict with the essence you are trying to achieve in the photo. In preparation for the shoot, try out some positions in front of a full-length mirror so that you have a complete view of your physical form.

A Shooting Session

I must confess that previously, my concept of a photo shoot came from movies like *Blow Up* where the fashion photographer is frantically snapping shots and yelling "yes, yes, more, give it to me!" as the model tosses her hair and writhes about in her skin-tight dress. But since then I've watched Tom work with an actress, directing her to establish a scene in her mind's eye, and it was more as if he were coaching her in an acting exercise.

Tom had told me he tries to establish a rapport at the look-see, explaining his approach to actors when they come to look over his portfolio. With the shoot I observed, it was obvious that this had happened, since the actress arrived already relaxed and up for the shoot. She brought changes appropriate to each of the three shots she wanted, and over coffee she discussed what she was after with Tom and Michael, the make-up artist. By the time Michael had her ready (keeping up a very funny monologue about growing up in Brooklyn as he made her up), almost a full hour had elapsed. Hair and make-up was set for the theatre shot first, keeping her hair fairly natural. (Later Michael gave it a little more body for the commercial shot, and then a sexy wave and more fullness for the soap shot. Make-up was also changed accordingly.) By this time she was very comfortable with Michael, Tom, the background music and the camera. Happy with how she looked and ready to start, she sat in front of a sort of drawing board which acted as a reflector but was also positioned so that she could lean on it.

Rather than trying to describe this in third person, I've transcribed a portion of that photo session from tape, to give you a sense of exactly how Tom "directs" an actor as he shoots. This is only a portion (maybe a third) of the shooting time, and there were other lapses of time to change hair and make-up, and just to relax as their conversation took a turn away from the photography. But I hope this will help you to create a working scenario for your own photo session. Notice how Tom's coaching is always directed toward the actress *creating a plan and including in it the person whom the camera has become.* An asterisk * indicates where he took photos.

Lean in, but don't sink in; not to be stiff, but think of your spine as being long and curving forward. Don't let this [upper torso] sag, because the minute this happens there's a passive quality to your body, that your face will always reflect. Look away from the camera, and get yourself involved in something in your own imagination, you're talking to someone, thinking about something, it doesn't matter what at all—just imagine that you hear someone approach, and come to the lens, keep the thoughts going on, just include the lens. The most important thing is that your have real thoughts going on. Taking all the time you want, imagine that you hear someone come into the room—the lens is the door—just include them. * Now, off camera imagine you hear the door open with a sudden noise, so it's a burst of energy. * Nice.

Now stay with the camera, as if you're looking down a street. In the distance you see someone coming toward you so that at first * there's an alertness that comes from someone looking vaguely familiar in the distance; as this person comes closer and closer, a slow recognition takes over. Make it someone you haven't seen in a while, think of someone real, that you like. Don't ever think about producing a smile, just think about the person and let an excitement build.* So that you're thinking about what you're going to do with this person...there's a plan that develops.*

[He talks her through this scenario a couple more times, taking several shots along the way]

Now, make it to a child, as if you're trying to tell this child with your eyes alone, 'look what I've got behind my back'—the beckoning. * Keep it to a child * 'come closer, come closer'. * Now think of something that you have just accomplished and you're really proud of, like your best audition, and a nice little chuckle, way down deep. Now the feeling of a great taste. Look away from the camera, get an image of a real special taste *or sensation, or special place; when the glow happens, just bring it back and share it. * So the action now is you're saying to this person here, guess what we're going to have to eat, or guess where I'm going to take you. * Make sure it doesn't get too serious or calculating. * I'm trying to get out a little of the little girl in you.*

*Try this—off camera again, good thoughts going on, hear a voice and anticipate who it is. There are three steps: you hear a voice that you haven't heard in a while; you look to the camera-'could it be?'; yes, it is! Be specific, make it a special person you haven't seen. Good * Try it again. * As you look to the camera, they aren't there yet, make it an open door, so when they come through it's a rush, a sudden glow takes over. **

*Keep to the camera, let a new idea take over - 'oh, that's what we'll do tonight!' * Now go back toward a great taste or a glow, and share it with this person. * Now with your hand out of view - you can use it to gesture if you want - say 'come here'. * That's the secret, to invite--no matter whether it's a serious or a commercial shot, it's to bring somebody closer to you. * Add the invitation, and it keeps the eyes brighter. Now someone's going to give you something, a gift. Now actually say 'For me?' * Now the thing to add is to wait for a response. Say it. * And the anticipation is almost pulling out of your chair--someone's holding out a $1,000 bill! **

*Now you're looking for yourself in a crowd scene in a movie; search for yourself; when you find yourself, you're surprised at what you see. You find yourself suddenly, and you're glad to see yourself, but you're doing something silly.**

[A break here to relax a bit, and change clothing, hair and make-up for the commercial shot.]

*Now, all the commercial shots are really inviting, so draw someone close to you; there's no subtext, the task is simply to pull someone toward you. So look away and back to the camera with just a 'come here, quick'. * Now try with something that ends with an 'e' - come with me.*

[Here the actress says she's been using her little nephew, Ricky, which ends in 'e']

*OK, 'come here, Ricky', and keep your eyes bright as you wait for him. * Ask a little question, like 'Wanna go to the beach, Ricky?' It's a question and something that's already fun. [several tries at this] * Always with excitement, you're ready to get out of the chair; you're acting as if you were his age.* That was a little generic, find a more specific invitation.* Watch him now, stay with it, and he's doing something enjoyable, encourage it. * Keep encouraging him. **

*Now this is your first commercial job. Keep it näive, there's no ulterior motive, just 'may I help you?' * Lock onto the camera with it. * This kind of mental activity is good to remember, because a commercial is always an invitation, you're pulling someone in. Sometimes commercial directors don't give you much to work with. Now don't let any sophistication leak in, you just want to help. * Avoid any doubts, make it positive—the slightest hint of doubt in your mind will read in your eyes as passive. * Now, try it with a child. You're a kindergarten teacher, say 'come with me' to something fun. * It's a question, not a command; the subtext here is 'you're gonna like it.' * Now you're the child, and go back to 'who, me?' - you've been chosen for something fun. * That's it, I could see you getting younger and younger. **

[After more similar work for the commercial shot, another break to change for her soap shot.]

*Now we can uncork all the subtext. Now, just keep it alive by again beckoning, but with a little mischievous purpose--you fill in the blank. Good. * That's the way, keep it bright, that's exactly it, * now, stretch around, right there, hold it, lovely. * Savor a great taste as you're doing it. Yummm. * A little evil fun again. Keep the same position, keep the fun, lighten it a bit, not quite as evil. A little more näive, but keep the same draw. * As if you're saying, 'c'mere'... with a little sex behind it * now closed lips and the draw; exactly * now have a little fun with it and let it grow slowly * let it become a laugh as you realize how ridiculous the situation is. **

[They repeated similar sequences with slight changes in body positions and lighting.]

*Now you're in a situation of extreme sexuality, just put on a totally innocent 'who, me?' but underneath there's fire. * Cover the sexuality, you're body is taking care of it, have fun with the innocence. * Now let a giggle come up very slowly.* Lean on your hand, without touching it much, now drop your hand.**

The session lasted about two hours total, one hour of preparation and an hour of shooting, with the changes as indicated. The actress left feeling great, and her optimism was confirmed when she picked up the contact sheet. In talking to Tom further about his "direction" he told me about photographing children, and how easy it is for them to "endow" the camera. He told one little boy to look for his dog in the camera lens, and when the child exclaimed "There he is! I see him!" Tom snapped an incredible picture that just jumped off the page at you. That's the kind of involvement you need to have with the camera to allow the photographer to capture that essence of *you* on film.

Choosing Your Pictures

Once you have your contact sheets, you can start the selection process. The sight of 72 or even 108 little reproductions of your face staring up at you can be intimidating at first, but your eye will probably jump towards the best of them pretty quickly. Photo #33 shows a proof sheet, and #34 shows the actress looking at it; as you can see, she's cut a square the size of one picture out of a sheet of white paper. This enables her to look at each picture individually, which is very different than seeing all of them at once. Using a photographer's *loupe* or a magnifying glass as you look at each picture will enable you to see how details will look when they are enlarged. First eliminate any pictures with your mouth open and your eyes shut, and the ones which only a mother could love. Next eliminate the ones that have technical imperfections like poor contrast, hard shadows, etc., using the same criteria as when you looked at the portfolio. With the remaining possibilities, look carefully for those that best bring out the qualities we've been talking about—the mystery and the invitation. Eliminate any in which you look tentative or doubtful. Your picture should be active, not passive, a moment when the face on the picture is going to come off the page and include the viewer in a special action. Now take them to *a few* friends, including a director or casting director if you can. But ultimately, rely on your own judgment—and don't be afraid to trust your first impressions.

What to do if, horror of horrors, you truly cannot find a picture that you like, or if you believe the technical quality is not acceptable? Well, if you did your research well, you know what the photographer's policy is. Since you are contracting a photographer with the understanding that you will come out with satisfactory photographs, one would hope s/he will offer some sort of a guarantee: a complete or partial reshoot for free, or at a reduced price. However, some photographers don't guarantee their work. In the course of your research, you determined your photographer's policy, and you decided it was one you could live with. If you are unhappy with your photos and the photographer says you will have to pay something extra for a reshoot, look very hard at the technical aspects of the contact sheet, perhaps even taking it to another professional for an opinion. Think about whether you believe this photographer *can* get an acceptable shot of you. It's awful to think of losing the money on the first session, but even worse to pay more for a second session and still be dissatisfied. If you feel the fault was more with you than the photographer, set up another shoot, and do more preparation this time—reconsider the clothes, the hair, the make-up and the subtext. In a worst case scenario—you don't like any of the shots, and there is no guarantee of any kind—you will just have to swallow the loss and work harder at finding a better photographer.

The great temptation, of course, is to settle for a photo that you're unhappy with, merely because of the financial investment it represents. I strongly advise you not to do that, because you're putting your career on hold for as long as you have a headshot that makes you uncomfortable. You will sabotage yourself with self-doubt, and the photo you paid so much for will be working against you. Yes, it's a lot of money, but *one commercial* that you may get if your photo is really good would make up for the loss. Ultimately, *the best way to avoid a contact sheet nightmare is to be thorough in all the research and preparation we've discussed.* Use the worksheets to organize yourself, and write everything down, especially if days or weeks may go by between selecting a photographer and getting a shooting date. If you've done your homework, there should be no question that you will end up with good photos.

When you have selected the photos you like from the contact sheet, you'll return the sheet to the photographer, telling him/her which ones you have selected and asking when the prints will be ready. At the hour agreed upon, you'll pick up your prints, *making sure that the photographer is going to be there when you do!* That's your assurance that the prints you pick up will be ready to go on to the next steps, the retouching and copying.

The photographer should have provided you with finished prints to your specifications on double weight rag paper (the type retouchers require), without dust spots, correctly cropped, with good contrast. It is most important that the original print that you get from the photographer be in correct contrast: black hair should have detail in it; very light skin should have tone. Reproductions generally *increase* the contrast (light goes lighter, dark goes darker) so these details are important. In general, since most reproduction prints will have more contrast than the original, the original should be just *slightly* on the soft side of ideal. In looking at the finished prints, consider all the points we discussed earlier in the section on looking at a portfolio. If part of your face washes out in a highlight, or your hair blends into the background, point it out to the photographer right there and then, and discuss what can be done in the printing process to correct the problem. Far better to wait a few more days to have a new print made than to spend more money on 100 copies of a photo with poor contrast.

Retouching and Reproduction

Once you have picked up the originals, the next question is retouching. The actor should be included in every step of the photo session, including the retouching. Retouching is *not* rebuilding your face to be more glamorous. You don't want to set yourself up for that embarrassing moment when you walk into the audition and the director does a double-take at the picture in her hand to be sure it's you. In the interest of presenting yourself as you really are, the only retouching you should do is to soften lines that normal photography will freeze into an unnatural hardness, and remove blemishes that are not permanent. One of the vagaries of photography is that it emphasizes darkness under the eyes and sharp lines around eyes and jowls; these are less noticeable in life because a face is in motion and the shadows are constantly changing. Because a photograph freezes and thus hardens them, they can legitimately be softened without loosing the integrity of the likeness.

The best kind of retouching is *etching*, where parts of the emulsion are removed with a sharp knife, as opposed to *air brushing*, which actually adds material to the picture. The etching process is progressive; it gradually takes off part of the emulsion, to continually produce lighter shades of gray. With airbrushing you're adding a layer, and it is likely to show in a copy. You should be able to discuss the specific retouching with either your photographer or the retoucher. Ideally, a plastic overlay is used and marks to be retouched are drawn in grease pencil right over the face. This overlay becomes a guide for the retoucher, who refers to it constantly. Most photographers don't have a retoucher in their studio, but can usually recommend somebody; or retouching can be done in the reproduction lab. Retouching generally costs about $25 per print. Try to speak directly to the person who will actually be doing the work, so nothing gets lost in translation.

Your final step is to have the original prints, now retouched, reproduced in quantity. The reproduction process involves rephotographing your original 8x10 to produce a large negative, which then is used to make inexpensive copies. This is called the *copy negative* or *reproduction negative*, or sometimes the *inter-negative*; usually a 5x7 or 8x10 negative. This is a critical point in the whole process, because it is in making the copy negative that skin tones or separate tones of the picture are copied or removed. Before the copies are run off from this negative, some labs offer a test print. It costs a little extra, but it's worth it. When inspecting the test print, look for the closest possible similarity to the original print in terms of contrast and skin tone. If you are having your name applied to the photo, this will be done to the original, before the copy negative is shot. Whether or not your lab offers a test, the finished product should be as close as possible to the original.

Prices vary widely among reproduction labs. They will all have representative photos for inspection, and it is well worth it to ask your friends for recommendations, and to shop around. Price is not necessarily an indicator of quality. The poor reproduction of your photograph can destroy the uniqueness that you and your photographer worked so hard to achieve.

The Final Product

Now that you've read all four chapters on the photo session, get started! Start on your Worksheets, and look through all the photos in here not once, but several times. Cart this book around with you when you go to look at friends' headshots, tuck it in a bag and take it with you on a look-see. You know all the tricks, now there's nothing to it but some hard work. Don't skimp on the preparation time for the shooting session. You know that feeling before you step on stage opening night that maybe you should have run your lines once more that afternoon? Don't show up at your session feeling under-prepared. Arrive confident and expecting to have fun, and you'll come out with a picture that makes you feel good when you hand it across the casting table.

How often must you go through this expensive ordeal? Don't believe a photographer who says flatly you will need a new one every year. It makes more sense to assume you will have to change your photo as often as you go through fairly radical changes in your life. If directors do a double-take at your picture as you walk in the door, or say your name questioningly to be sure you're really the person in the picture they're looking at, consider a new photo. But remember that a picture with real personality lasts longer than one without, because you're relying on the inner self, not just the physical self.

Peter Fletcher

Laura MacDermott

Photos 1 & 2 - *Typical NYC headshots. Borderless, most of picture taken up by face. Neutral background with names on front: #1 in "knockout" (black type in white box), #2 in "reverse" (white letters on black).*

Jennifer Jacoby

Photo 3 - *Portrait style photo, with black line around frame, now becoming fashionable. A little more body shown, arms and hands. Name printed in border.*

Photo 4 - *Typical L.A. shot. More body shown. Natural background, shot outside in soft overcast light. No name on front.*

Photo 5 - Commercial. *Bright, enthusiastic, uncomplicated. Inviting all viewers to share her excitement. Hair and make-up simple, clean, not heavy. Clothing casual, open collar.*

Photo 6 - Upscale Commercial. *Open and inviting, but more businesslike invitation. Clothing more professional, tailored.*

These show the range possible from one photo session with make-up & hair stylist.

Photo 7 - Soap. *Heaviest make-up and styled hair. The invitation is full of intrigue. Sexy. Clothes and jewelry glamorous.*

Photo 8 - Legit/Film. *Intelligent, confident. The invitation is more personal. A little twinkle of mystery in the expression. Make-up even and natural. Suggests a mind at work.*

Photo 9 - *Bad shirt: white, no detail in the fabric. The eye goes to the whitest part of the print, de-emphasizing the face. Can make the face look fat.*

Photo 10 - *Bad shirt: black, no detail in the fabric. When copies are made, it will be a big, black void at the bottom. Isolates the head.*

Photo 11 - *Don't fall for the "natural" look. Headshots need make-up to define and draw features together. Proper hair and make-up <u>present</u> you to the viewer.*

Photo 12 - *Heavy make-up on men makes the face too uniform, too pretty, obscures natural skin texture. Use only enough to soften a heavy beard, hide blemishes, or lighten eye bags.*

Photo 13 - *Too much front light. Overexposed. Shows no details of features.*

Photo 14 - *High contrast. Soft shades of gray are reduced to pure black and white.*

These two pages show some of the most

Phot 17 - *No reflector. Some light must be reflected or flashed from below, to fill in chin and eye shadows.*

Photo 18 - *Too shadowy. Light very angular for "dramatic effect." Hard shadows create the suspicion that you are hiding scars or weight.*

Photo 15 *- Low contrast. Too gray, muddy; no blacks or whites, no sparke.*

Photo 16 *- Correct contrast. Grays are in their correct proportion.*

common lighting and printing mistakes.

Photo 19 *- Too much hair light. Makes blonde hair look white, dark hair looks gray. There should be just enough to separate head from background.*

Photo 20 *- Good all around lighting and contrast. The face is "present," naturally shaded, and separated from the background.*

Photo 21 - *Background too dark. Behind dark hair, the head recedes, melts into the distance. Copies make it far worse.*

Photo 22 - *Properly lit for Black actor. Skin has real tone gradations, not too light or dark. Hair separated from background.*

Photo 23 - *A typical studio set-up: in front, an umbrella or box-diffuser; reflector on table in front; hair light above; background medium gray with light on the bottom to give it bounce.*

Photo 24 - *Don't fall for special effects. Soft focus, grainy, cute filters or bizarre cropping don't make you "memorable"...they make you weird.*

Photo 25 - *Pretty face, but passive, slightly doubtful. The "idea" in her mind hasn't yet included the viewer.*

Photo 26 - *Here her choice is to include the viewer. Her confidence radiates. She has the twinkle of an idea about to be shared.*

Expressions.

Photo 27 - *Not unpleasant, but unspecific. Just like acting, find a verb which includes the viewer in a present action.*

Photo 28 - *His excitement is specific and his "plan" requires this viewer for its completion.*

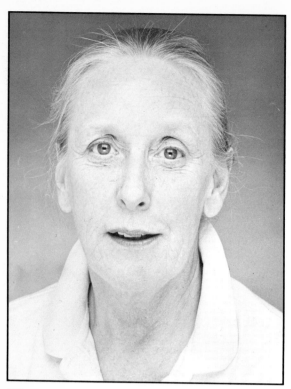

Photo 29 - *A passive, uninvolved expression. Avoid "wary" or "doubtful" looks.*

Photo 30 - *Excitement and specific ideas involve the viewer.*

More expressions.

Photo 31 - *Passive or private thoughts exclude the viewer, are one step from being hostile.*

Photo 32 - *Directness, intelligence, with a hint of a "plan," make the most memorable photos (despite breaking all the rules with his black turtleneck).*

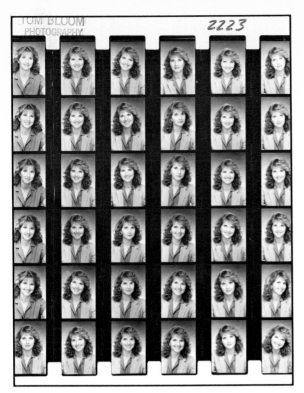

Photo 33 - *A typical proof sheet.*

Photo 34 - *Proofs should be inspected with a magnifier or "loupe" and a paper cut-out to isolate individual pictures.*

Photo 35 - *Cropped too close. No sense of this actress' body or neckline.*

Photo 36 - *Cropped too far. Head becomes too small to dominate the photo. Remember, you are selling your face.*

Photo 37 - The retoucher, Toni Weissman, at work. Through a magnifier she "etches" the surface of the print with a sharp knife to lighten dark lines or areas.

Photo 38 - An unretouched photo.

Photo 39 - An over-retouched photo.

Photo 40 - Correctly retouched photo. Eyes are brightened, a few lines are eliminated or softened. But not so much as to remake the face, or change the age.

Photo 41

Photo 42

A gallery of different actors, and photos which suggest their particular personalities.

Photo 43

Photo 44

Photo 45

Photo 46

A gallery of different actors, and photos which suggest their particular personalities.

Photo 47

Photo 48

Chapter 5

The Flip Side – Your Resume

At the instant that you read this chapter title and the word "resume" registered on your brain, you probably began to worry about how "good" your credits are. That's the main concern of most actors when they think about the resume side of their P/R, and of course it's a valid one, because the strength of your credits has a bearing on how you look to a casting person. But right now it's *misplaced* concern, because your credits are an unalterable fact of the moment; you can't change your credits for the sake of your resume any more than you can change the shape of your ears for your photo. So the object of this chapter is to learn to accept those credits, like your ears, as your unique self and to see how you can present them in the best possible light. We'll talk about general format and content first, and then get to more specifics on the "graphic image" you'll use to present yourself.

What I describe in the following pages is the standard format for a theatrical resume, set up in an outline form as opposed to a paragraph. Some actors prefer a paragraph, (and in fact some agencies insist on a paragraph), so I have included a sample of one in Resume F, page 50. I'm not enamored of paragraphs because they've always struck me as a little pretentious, rather like a mini press release. That's just personal opinion, and apparently some agents and casting people feel they're easier to read (they are generally only about 15-20 lines). The paragraph makes sense for a well-known actor, but in general I believe the standard layout gives more information in an easily digestible format, if correctly put together. If you decide to use a paragraph form, or if an agent insists on it, you should put it together as you would a bio for a program. If this is your agency's policy, they will probably want it on their letterhead, with your name typed in caps and your vital stats, then the paragraph in the middle of the page. If it's a good agency, by all means go along with them, since they're the ones who are selling you to casting people. That said, we'll go back to discussing the more standard resume format.

Vital Statistics

While each resume, like a photo, is unique to the individual, there is a generally accepted format that follows a very simple logic: you put the most critical information closest to the top. Think of your name and vital statistics as the "headline" and the first few credits as the "lead paragraph" in a newspaper article; if they catch the interest of the reader—and if they meet the specific needs of the casting person—then the rest of your credits, your training and special skills will be read also.

Start off your resume with your name, union affiliations, contact phone number and talent agent, if represented. Obviously, your name should be the one you intend to use as your professional name; when you join a union you will be told if it is an acceptable name, belonging to no one else already a union member. If not, you will have to alter it to make it acceptable. Sometimes this can be done by use of a middle name or initial, but some actors find it necessary or desirable to adopt a professional name. If that's the case, don't be tempted to get too clever, since you'll have to live with it for a long time.

Some performers like to categorize themselves as an Actor, Singer and/or Dancer, in a line just below their name. This is a matter of choice, but you should realize that you are categorizing yourself not only by what you choose to call yourself, but also by what you choose *not* to call yourself. Here are what those categories mean to me as a director when I'm looking through P/R's:

- Actor - does not sing or dance with any confidence, don't cast in musical (or Chorus only, if some singing ability is indicated elsewhere on resume).

- Singer - legit, cabaret or chorus, depending on resume; not as comfortable with acting roles, not a dancer.

- Dancer - use in musical as specialty dancer or dancing chorus part that doesn't require strong voice.

- Actor/Singer - consider for any musical or non-musical role.

- Singer/Actor - consider primarily for musical roles, should be capable of musical leads.

- Singer/Dancer - consider for Chorus parts.

- Actor/Singer/Dancer - genuine "triple threat," probably would lean more toward casting in musicals, unless credits show many good roles in non-musical plays too.

If you label yourself, you'd better be able to come through in that area. If you're just starting off, and you're still expanding your skills, it's probably better not to add a label yet. On the other hand, if you're a real "triple threat" and your credits prove it, then flaunt it. And if you know you're not capable as a singer and don't want to be called in for musicals, then just "Actor" will usually keep you in the pile for non-musical shows.

Generally it is not necessary, and not necessarily wise, to have a home address or home phone number listed. Once you send out a resume, there is no knowing what can happen to it (as a matter of fact, some turn up on Manhattan sidewalks, among street vendors' piles of used books and magazines), and for your own protection it is best to list a service phone only. If you use an answering machine at your home instead of a service, the message on the machine should be businesslike and should avoid any nonessential information about the household. If you are signed with an agency, they may want your resume printed on their letterhead, or they may give you the agency's logo to have printed on your resume; or at the very least, you will list your agent's name and the agency phone number as your contact. If you are freelancing with an agency, they will stamp the agency's name and phone number on your resume every time they submit you, or they may stick their label over your service number, to assure that when you are submitted by that agency the casting person will call them rather than calling you directly.

If you are a student, sending out P/R's looking for summer jobs or internships, you might want your address on the resume, in case it becomes separated from your cover letter. You might even need two addresses and phone numbers, at school and at a permanent residence (label them as such). You should be confident that anyone who has your P/R will be able to get in touch with you, not just until the end of the semester, but into the foreseeable future. And you should also be sure that any telephone number listed on your resume will be answered in your absence by a machine or by a responsible person, not by a lackadaisical roommate who doesn't own a pencil. I would suggest, however, that once you settle in the city you'll be using as your home base, you remove all but your service number from your resume.

Vital statistics should generally include height, weight, eyes and hair color, as it is necessary for the casting person to have immediate reference to these factors. Some women who are quite tall leave off the height, as do some men who are quite short. Some actors who are a little overweight either understate their weight or leave it off entirely. This follows the same theory as not showing poor teeth in a commercial shot: get the audition first so they can see you act, then let the casting person decide if your height or weight or teeth really matter that much. The only problem with that practice is that some casting people get very cranky when they feel an actor has deliberately misrepresented him/herself on the P/R. That's why I believe many casting people will begin to favor the portrait style photo that shows more body—although an actor who wishes to hide physical attributes is still going to opt for a headshot.

It is not necessary to list your age or age range if you have a good picture; let the casting person decide whether you look the right age for the part. Listing a range is too tricky—what's the difference between 24-32 and 25-31? And if the range is too large (I've seen 25-60 listed as a range) it looks as though you have a very unrealistic understanding of the casting business. Of course, if you look 20 in your photo and 35 when you walk in the door, the casting director is going to be understandably disturbed, but the first four chapters of this book should help you avoid that. An exception to this rule is that if you are a minor (under 18) you should put your date of birth on your resume. There are special work-related rules that producers must follow when dealing with minors, and the casting people must know that you're under 18. Put your date of birth rather than age (since the age will change, but the date of birth won't); then when you become a "major" at age 18, remove it.

Measurements or clothing sizes need be listed only in modeling or commercial resumes; again for your own privacy and protection, leave measurements to the costume designer after you have the role. Including your social security number is optional, since it's not needed until you're hired for a job, although some agents prefer that their clients put it on the resume. With recent tightening of immigration laws, you might want to include "U.S. Citizen" or "Naturalized Citizen" if you were not born in this country.

If you can sing at all, giving some information on your voice is a good idea. Even though you may not be a "Singer" or an "Actor/Singer," if there is no mention of vocal range, and no musical credits, the assumption is that you're tone deaf. If you can carry a tune, and could sing chorus or handle a song as part of the action in a non-musical play, put your voice range—soprano, alto, tenor, baritone, bass—in the vital statistics section of your resume. If you have trained as a singer and can confidently type yourself as "legit" "belt" or "pop," do so, as this will indicate more than a passing knowledge of singing—but if you put it down, you'd better be able to come through! Some singers may even give a precise musical range, i.e. "21/2 octave range" or "belt to B above middle C." Or you can even notate your range on a musical staff, drawn in proportion to the other information in this section. The indications you give in the stats should be further elaborated by your musical credits and training, so that the extent of your singing ability and casting potential in musicals is clearly evident on your resume.

Credits

The section that lists your credits is usually organized by genre: "Theatre," "Film," "Television", etc. If you have sufficient diverse experience, you may want to break "Theatre" down into subsections like Broadway, National Tours, Off-Broadway, Showcase, Stock, Regional, etc. Or you may want to distinguish simply between "New York" (which can encompass Showcases, Off- and Off-Off-Broadway) and "Regional & Stock." Which category comes first on the resume depends on where you are based, where your emphasis as a performer is, and where your best credits are. If you work a good deal in more than one genre, you may even want to have two resumes with different layouts, so that your "Film & TV" resume would list those credits first, while your theatrical resume would have the theatre credits first (see resumes D and E, page 51).

There are a variety of approaches to the credits section on a resume, but one basic tenet holds: include the information that makes you look the best, *but don't lie.* Even setting aside the questionable ethics, the theatre world is too small, and you're too likely to get caught. I personally know of several instances where actors were caught lying on their resumes, always with such a negative impact on the performer that it certainly wasn't worth the lie. One such incident occurred in a combined audition with thirty producers present. As one woman finished her 3-minute audition and left the stage, a producer rose and addressed the rest of us: "This actress lists my company on her resume, and I want you all to know that she has never worked for me, in the plays she lists or in any others. This is a complete fabrication." Do you think the producers in the audience believed anything else on her resume, after hearing that?

Of course, there's a lot of gray area between out and out lying and stretching the truth a bit. Before you yield to the temptation to list a role that you only understudied, picture an audition where the director says to you, "That's odd—I saw that production. In fact, as I recall it, my best friend played that role." An understudy role should be listed as such: "understudy" or "u/s" with a further notation "performed twice" or whatever, if you actually went on in the role.

Remember that most people who look at resumes look at *a lot* of resumes, and know all the tricks of fattening up slim credits. The heading "Representative Roles" is a transparent camouflage for "roles I did in scene study class" or "roles I would like to play," and therefore is relatively meaningless. Don't use that heading for roles you actually performed; use the headings previously mentioned and list the names of the theatres too. One stretch used often by students, which I consider harmless if somewhat futile, is to use the name of the theatre itself, rather than the institution, on college credits. Thus, a play performed while attending Williams College becomes credited to "Adams Memorial Theatre, Williamstown, MA." The hope is that it might sound like a professional production—perhaps they'll think you performed at the Williamstown Theatre Festival, which uses the same space in the summer. This type of prevarication won't get by too many seasoned resume readers—in the case given, for example, we know that anyone who's worked professionally at Williamstown Theatre Festival will use that name on their resume. But it's relatively harmless, and if you think it makes your resume look better, go ahead and try it.

A similar stretch is the practice of trying to camouflage a community theatre production so it sounds like a professional credit. Personally, I have some sympathy with this cause. There are many times when a good solid community theatre production is higher quality work than an under-rehearsed, thrown together "professional" workshop. Why should a lead role that you worked on for eight weeks and brought to full bloom in production be given less weight than a twenty-minute scene study in an acting workshop? But the fact of the matter is that most people reading resumes (myself included) tend to give more credence to *any* type of professional credit than to community theatre productions. So here is one place where I'd say it's fine to try to disguise the non-professional nature of the company, especially if you carried a lead. Drop the words "community" or "civic" from sight and list the theatre building rather than the name of the group, if need be, i.e., "Dodd Theatre Center" rather than "Doddsville Community Players".

The critical point is that your resume should represent your actual experience: the role, the play and the theatre where you played it, possibly including the director of the production. The last is important not only to give credence to your resume, but because directors may pick up on mutual acquaintances, which gives you something to talk about at an audition or interview, and makes you more memorable. Whether you list all the directors you've worked under, or perhaps just the better known ones, is a choice you should make based on the impressiveness of the list and the overall look it will give to the layout. Don't crowd the credits with names that will probably not be recognized—in those cases the name and location of the theatre company is sufficient—but if you have worked with well known directors, you should show it. It is not necessary to list playwrights' names, unless it is a new play and you want to emphasize that fact.

If you are just entering the professional world from a training school, obviously your credits are going to be limited. Make the most of what you've done, but don't try to stretch it too far. List any professional credits, like summer stock, before your school credits. Try to give a positive (but honest) picture of the type of work you did in school, and list any guest directors who might be known outside of your school. Casting people will pay more attention to your training credits in this case, because it will be obvious that you haven't had much professional experience. Be flexible in your thinking. When you're just starting out, an Apprenticeship with an Equity company might be your only professional credit, so you'll list everything you did there as a credit, showing even understudy roles. As you add professional credits, you can drop the understudy roles, and eventually list the Apprenticeship under "Training."

If you are young, should you list high school credits? Generally not. The exception might be if you attended a specialized school like the High School of Performing Arts, or if you received some noteworthy award, like the Irene Ryan Award. If you really have no other credits than high school, get some fast, because you simply will not be able to compete in this market, against people of a similar age who started drama camp at 7 and did their first season of stock at 14. Find a nearby professional company and work as an Intern or Apprentice doing anything at all, so you can show at least one contact with a professional theatre. If you're looking for TV, commercial or film work, get some kind of exposure in front of a camera, even if only for a local cable channel or a student film. And then as soon as you have acquired a reasonable number of professional credits drop your high school credits entirely.

Film, TV and Commercial Credits

Generally a New York actor's resume will list theatre credits first, while an L.A. actor's resume will list Film and TV credits first. As we indicated earlier, it is certainly possible to have two resumes with different layouts, and this is a good solution for an actor who is "bicoastal" and is being submitted in both cities. The resumes are essentially the same, but the theatre and film/tv sections are reversed. Examples can be found on page 51 in Resumes D and E.

List a film or TV credit by the title of the film, your role in it and the production company. Soap credits should be listed with the name of the soap, the name of the character if it had one, and the network. If you don't list a name, the casting director assumes it was an extra or "under 5". Some actors make up a name for their character when they play an "under 5" and list that name on their resume. According to Jean Rohn at *All My Children*, this can be an embarrassment at an interview, because the casting director assumes a role with a name is at least a "day player," and if the actor is asked about it and has to confess it was actually an extra or under 5, it sounds like padding the resume (which it is, of course). Some actors feel they shouldn't list extra parts at all, but Jean stressed the importance of indicating whatever experience they have had on camera.

Regarding this last point: all the film, television and commercial casting people I spoke to felt that good theatrical credits were a real plus for an actor seeking work on camera. By the same token, however, working before a camera is so different than stage work, it is reassuring to the casting director to see some on-camera experience on a resume. For that reason actors should list whatever they can, including student films, if they are just beginning to acquire film/tv credits. NYU student films in New York and UCLA films in L.A., for example, are perfectly valid credits—some films produced by students in both places have even won awards at various festivals. Actors arriving in either city without film credits would do well to pursue roles in student films, to get some camera work on their resume as soon as possible. Even listing a student film at Podunk U. shows that you know which end of the lens to act in front of. The rule again is to drop these credits as you add more professional ones.

Timing

Unlike work resumes in the "real world" where you list your most recent job first and work back through the years, on a theatrical or film resume you ignore the date of the credit, and list your most important credits first regardless of when you did them. Do not list any dates, as this will just clutter up the list of credits. When you played a role has little bearing on anything; the fact that you did play it is what counts.

The only time you might take exception to this general rule is if you are re-entering the business after a hiatus in your career. If you are working steadily over a long period of time, you will drop credits from your resume as you age out of their range. But if a woman had an active career in her twenties, then stopped acting for ten years to raise a family and wants to begin acting again in her late thirties, her best credits may be fifteen years too young for her current age. A forty-year old picture on the back of credits like Juliet or Jill Tanner in *Butterflies are Free* looks a little ludicrous. What to do?

I advise that you take the direct approach: make it clear that there is a gap of several years in your credits, and *why* (see Resume C on page 48 for an example). Include on your resume a brief statement to the effect that you made two positive choices: one to exit the business for a duration, to fulfill "x" (be "x" mother or fatherhood, world travel, or a career as a public defender) and now another one to come back in. As an indication of the type of work you were doing in your first career, list your very best credits and leave it at that—don't drag up everything from high school on. List your recent credits since you started back in, even if they're limited to a few. Make sure the time periods are distinct on your layout, so it doesn't look like you played the ingenue parts last year, at 42. List your training and special skills, drawing on whatever you did with your life during the hiatus to contribute to your value as an actor. And most of all, *don't fret about the gap!* If you're re-entering in your forties, remember that you've outlasted all the actors who burned out and gave up for good when they hit 35. You'll find the competition has greatly decreased in your age range. Let the current 23-year-old's fight it out among themselves for the young hotshot roles; there are many opportunities in commercials, TV and film, and if you're willing to leave town for six weeks regional theatres will welcome you with open arms.

Training

The training section should summarize your education if you went to a college or university, and should identify your training in acting and related skills. As a general rule, as your credits increase in impressiveness, the importance of your training section decreases. If you've been performing leads with major theatre companies or if you have Broadway credits, the school you went to is immaterial. If you're just starting out, maybe you haven't too much to offer other than good solid training. But try to keep the training section proportionally smaller than the credit section anyway, so it doesn't appear that since no one will hire you to act, you just keep taking classes.

If you have an advanced degree, list it. If it's a major theatrical training institution, you can almost leave it at that: "M.F.A. in Acting, Yale School of Drama" says all you need to say. If it's a lesser known school, but you studied with a well-known faculty member or guest director, work that name in somehow; you might work it in under credits, if for instance Liviu Ciulei was a guest director in your junior year and cast you in his show.

Use the training section also to emphasize the special training you have in various areas like acting, dance, voice (as in vocal technique for the stage), singing (as in singing), commercial or film technique, etc. Should you list all your teachers by name? Not necessarily, though you might want at least one name next to each area of training. But remember that which names you list as directors or teachers is dependent not on how much you liked them or even how much you learned from them, but whether their name will be recognized by the people looking at your resume. If you have trained with teachers well-known in their field or in the city where you're looking for work, include their names; if the names are not well known, and they clutter the resume, then simplify it by just listing the type and amount of training. The purpose of this section is twofold: first, to let the casting person know where (and with whom, if applicable) you trained, hoping that s/he will be impressed by the institution's reputation, or may even have a personal connection there; secondly, to display the areas and extent of your training in acting, voice, dance, and related skills.

Special Skills

For a few years there was a computerized resume service in New York called RoleCall. They installed terminals in casting directors' offices, and actors paid an annual fee to have their resume entered into the system. One of the features of the system was to sort actors by special skill, so that a casting director who needed someone who played the lute could ask the computer and get a list of actors who were also lute players. I've always liked the idea, and am willing to bet it will reappear. Until it does, casting people continue to keep such lists in their heads or their file cabinets. To help them out, you'll list your special skills in the last section of your resume.

The idea is to show any special talents you have that might be useful in film or commercial work, or that could be an extra attraction to a theatre company. Start with acting-related skills like dialects, stage combat, mime or acrobatics. Include proficiency with musical instruments and athletic abilities, especially individual sports like horseback riding or swimming. Include whether you drive a car (standard and/or automatic), motorcycle, truck. You can add to the list almost anything you do well, like photography, graphic design, American Sign Language, carpentry, electronics, etc. The list of skills that could be useful to a theatre company or in a particular commercial or industrial film is almost endless, and these things too can generate conversation at an interview or audition. Be selective, however, about what you include. You don't want the list to be too long, or the individual skills get lost. Try to include those things that you do really well and *that could prove useful* to the casting director.

If you have a "second career" in theatre, you may want to indicate it by saying "Directing resume on request" or "Technical resume on request," but do so only if you are genuinely willing to work in those areas. If you are non-Equity and looking for any job in theatre, it can be a plus for you to show other skills, because many non-Equity companies, particularly summer companies, are looking for multi-skilled people. If you are still in school and don't have a lot of credits, you can include non-acting credits right on your resume, perhaps even setting up a special section for them. However, once you can present a full acting resume, if you want to be considered for acting positions only you should not include your non-acting experience on a resume.

To help you decide what to include in your special skills section, think about the things you've watched actors do on commercials lately. In addition to driving abilities and individual sports, "good with babies" or with children, or animals, is a plus. Actors who have been used in print jobs as hand or foot models should indicate it on their resume; if you own your own formal wear you can list something like "extensive formal wardrobe" (this is desirable in casting extras and under-fives). Character voices and dialects should definitely be included. Oddities like "playing spoons" or "Woody Woodpecker imitation" can be added at your discretion, according to your abilities. Some casting people will be amused or intrigued, while others may be turned off by anything too cute. Whatever you put down though, if you say you can do it, you'd better be able to come through on the spot if asked.

Before we leave the content of your resume and go on to layout, there are a few things you should *not* include. A theatrical resume should not have a statement of your goals, as you might find on a resume for a "real job." Everyone who looks at your resume knows your goal is to get an acting job, so it's redundant and unprofessional. Nor is your resume the proper place for your theory of acting, or for reviews. If you want to create a separate sheet of reviews on your work to send out with your resume, that's fine, but including them on the resume looks amateurish. In the chapters on photos we talked a great deal about how you can create a photo that reflects your personality and shows how you are unique. The purpose of the resume side is to market yourself via your credits, and to show that you are a capable business person as well as a competent professional actor. Something of your personality will come through by virtue of where you have worked and what type of training you have sought, and your special skills say something about you as well. The layout, which we'll get to in a moment, will reflect your personal taste also, but the primary thing a resume should say to the beholder is *this actor is a professional*.

Graphic Image

Consider your resume not only a source of information, but your *graphic image*. Everyone in the advertising field knows the importance of the visual impact of an ad, and it's a good exercise for an actor to think of a resume as a display advertisement when determining how to lay out the information on it. When casting, one goes through literally hundreds of resumes, and they, even more than photos, have an uncanny ability to numb the mind of the beholder after a while. So you should strive for a resume layout that is appealing to the eye, easy to read and emphasizes your strengths.

If you're not quite comfortable with the idea of a graphic image, try this experiment. First, look through the advertisements in a newspaper, maybe even a trade paper like *Back Stage*. Lay the paper open and get far enough away from it so you can't really read the smaller print in the ads, and notice which ads on a given page pull your eye toward them. Study those ads and determine what it is about the layout and composition, aside from catchy copy, that draws focus. [Note: when I refer to *layout* I'm talking about the arrangement of words (copy) and white space, or the shapes that your information will make on the page; by *composition* I mean the use of different typefaces, lines or borders that you may use to give emphasis or clarity to the copy.] After you've done this with several pages of ads, try it with resumes. Lay out a bunch of them together (or go to a copy center, where they have a display of resumes) and step back far enough so you can't actually read the credits. Which ones draw your eye, and why? In looking at the resumes, you'll realize that one doesn't have the same range of choices as with ads. You probably won't be using any photos or illustrations, and there is a fairly standard format for the body. But you do still have many resources at your disposal: type style and size, lines and borders, grouping and white space.

The most frequent mistakes made in setting up a resume are fairly simple ones. Poor layouts are those that are crowded together too tightly (hard to read), have too much white space (looks like you have no credits) or have equal spacing everywhere (also hard to read). Poor composition includes using a poor typewriter, one with an old ribbon and characters that are "dirty" (i.e., the space on the 'e' is filled in) or badly aligned; type that is too small or too crowded or all one size with no underlining or boldfacing. Any of these faults will make the resume boring or difficult to read, and will harm your presentation.

Working with print is an art in itself and beyond the scope of this book, but here are a few guidelines to help you talk with whomever does your resume. Type comes in many different styles, or typefaces. Some of them belong to the Roman or *serif* family, which means they have lines at the base of their letters (like the typeface of this book). Others are *sans serif*, or without those little lines, which gives a more contemporary appearance. In general, typefaces with serifs are easier to read, because the little lines keep the eye flowing from one letter to the next. Sans serif type, however, tends to be more condensed—you can get more characters in the same space because you don't have to allow room for the serifs. Within each different type style, you can add emphasis to a given word or heading with **Boldface** (a heavier version of the same type style), *Italic* (a slanted version) or ***Boldfaced Italic*** (you guessed it). Another way of adding emphasis is to increase the type size, which is measured in *points*. A good readable size for the body of your resume is 12 point type, which is the type size of this book and most of the sample resumes. As a rule, don't use any type smaller than 10 point. And you want to be sure the spacing between lines of type (called *leading*) is great enough so that the characters don't run into each other—the *descenders* like "y" shouldn't touch the *ascenders* like "h".

So with all the possible combinations of different type styles, faces and sizes, you could choose from thousands of ways to compose the text on your resume. But it doesn't need to be that confusing, because generally on a document as small as a resume, you don't want to mix type styles, so you'll pick out a serif type like

New Century Schoolbook (used in this book), or

Times Roman (so named because the *NY Times* uses it), or

Courier (IBM typewriters use this one) or

Palatino (a very graceful, light style).

Or you may choose a sans serif style like

Helvetica (a fairly condensed type), or

Avant Garde Gothic (this one spreads out more).

You'll create eye-catching headings with a slightly larger type (1-4 points larger than the body), or boldface, or Italic, or a combination thereof. Your name might be set in 20-24 point type, or you might even use a completely different typeface for your name and run it nearly the full width of the page. Look at the sample resumes and notice the different looks a resume can have, according to the typeface used.

Regarding layout, you'll set your name at the very top of the page, with your vital statistics below it, to one or both sides. Next come your credits, under the headings that make the most sense for you, as we discussed. The largest portion of space on your resume should be that devoted to the credits, say between 50% and 75% of the total area. Here you'll use columns for the play, role, theatre and/or director; or the film/program, role and producer for your film/TV credits. The lower 10-25% of the page will hold your education, training and special skills. Lines can be used very effectively to set off different sections. If you look at Resume B on page 49, you'll see an example of another use of lines: a box at the bottom of the resume labeled "Recent Credits." It's an option I like because it will keep your resume looking neat, giving you space to write new credits in as they happen without cramming them in haphazardly.

And it also projects the idea that you're constantly working. Of course, you always want to have something written in that space, so when you have your resume printed, leave a recent credit off of it! This is also a good way to call special attention to upcoming readings or workshops which you hope the casting people might attend.

The six sample resumes at the end of this chapter show various layouts for various purposes or at different points in these actors' careers. Layouts are limited only by your imagination and your printer's capabilities—and, one hopes, your good taste. Some interesting variations I've seen recently include:

- A line up the entire left margin of the resume, topped by a flower design. Printed in red ink on lavender paper, it was striking, but the ink color wasn't quite dark enough for a good contrast, and so it was difficult to read.

- A green border around all four sides, with the actor's name centered in bold caps, also printed in green, with the resume printed in black type. It was very eye-catching, and one could have a large run of the paper done with just the colored border and name, then print the resume in runs of 100, as needed. That way the expense of the second color is only swallowed once.

- A headshot *screened* (printed faintly) on white 8x10 paper, with a red line edging the screened image, and a 1/4" white border around the outside of the red line. The resume was superimposed in black over top of the screened photo, and a space was left blank at the bottom, under the heading "recent credits". Memorable, but expensive.

- A 11/4" wide strip of 6 different small photos made to look like a strip of film, sprocket holes and all, running down the left side of the resume. The photos were taken in various costumes: policeman, cook, construction worker, leather jacket, etc. Same idea as a composite, but much cheaper. This was run on a copier, however, so the images are streaky; it would take a more expensive print job to get them really sharp.

- Many examples of interesting composition and graphics (many of which are certainly home computer-generated, as we'll discuss in a moment) such as monograms, lines to set off the actor's name, fancy borders, etc.

Printing your Resume

Unless you've been asleep for the last ten years, you realize that we've experienced an incredible advance in "personal printing technology" (to coin a phrase, in case no one else thought of calling it that). In other words, it's now possible for the ordinary person, even the starving-actor-type ordinary person, to have access to reasonably priced printing for all occasions. That's the good news. The bad news is that since it's now so accessible, anything less looks tacky. In other words, I'm sorry, but typing your resume yourself on the manual typewriter you got when you went to college is simply not good enough. It's not even good enough to type it on the computer you younger folks got when you went to college, if it looks like "computer print." I'm not saying that such resumes will be discarded entirely by the casting people—necessarily—but they simply will not compete in terms of professional image.

The minimum acceptable standards for a resume to compete in today's market (in my opinion) is one typed on an electronic typewriter or word-processor with a letter-quality printer, and preferably with the capability of boldfacing text. For those of you unfamiliar with these terms, I'll explain that there are three kinds of printers that go with word-processors (computers): *dot matrix*, which spits little dots of ink on the paper to produce what one generally thinks of as "computer printing"; *letter quality*, which uses a little wheel of type striking through a ribbon like a typewriter, and *laser printers*, which are beyond my power of comprehension, but which turn out materials that look "printed" and can do fancy graphics. To further complicate things, there are dot matrix printers that spit out so many dots that the resulting print approaches that of the letter quality or even laser. These are OK for resumes, but the dot matrix printers where the print still looks like dots are not. Moreover, with the letter quality printer, make sure that it has a ribbon which is either *film* or *multi-strike* rather than nylon. These are just like typewriter ribbons, and nylon will give a fuzzier result than the other two, even if the nylon ribbon is new. Are you still wondering what's wrong with the IBM Selectric typewriter you can use during your lunch hour at the office where you're working as a temp? Nothing, except that it won't boldface, and it won't store your resume, so you'll have to completely retype it every time you add credits. If your office has an electronic machine, however, with a memory and boldfacing capabilities, use it—and as soon as you're making enough as an actor to quit the temp job, buy your own computer.

So, now that you comprehend the personal printing technology revolution, how do you get your resume printed? If you have your own computer with a letter quality or laser printer, you're all set, and you can update your resume as often as you like, just for the cost of the copies. If you a computer but your printer isn't good enough, take your disk to a friend or service and have the resume run off on their laser printer. That way the resume is still on your own disk which you can update as needed. If you are thinking of buying a computer, the type of printer should be a major consideration. Spend the extra money it takes to produce a professional looking page or you're missing the point of having a computer. If you don't have a computer of your own, perhaps you have a friend who does. But if you have a friend do your resume for you, make sure he's planning to stick around for a while, or that if he goes away he gives you the disk. What good is your friend with a computer if they're both in Idaho when you need your resume updated? Also, if you or your friend are doing your resume, make sure you lay it out in an 8"x10" format, not 81/2"x11". Copy services that commonly do theatrical resumes have special 8x10 paper; if yours doesn't, have them trim the copies to size.

If you don't have a computer or a friend with one, then look for a resume service. You will find that many places which copy photos also do resumes. Look at resume samples, and ask to see the typefaces, lines, borders, etc., that are available. You also should determine exactly how cheap and easy they will make it for you to update your resume. The harder and more expensive it is, the less likely you are to redo your resume as often as you should—which is as often as your credits change significantly, or when you find the handwritten additions threaten to take over. Ask if your resumes will be done on a copier or an offset printer. For quantities of 100, offset printing offers higher quality and consistency for the same or only slightly higher cost than copying. However, if the copier is top quality you may not even see any difference.

Use the Planning Schedule and Copy Service Comparison worksheets to keep track of your options, and select the best looking resume for the price you're willing to pay. Some actors like to have their resumes printed on ivory, colored or textured *stock* (the kind of paper used in a print job). If you like the look and want to spend the money, fine, it can make your resume stand out. But a good quality white stock is sufficient as long as the resume is well laid out. If you use a place which is not accustomed to doing theatrical resumes, you must again be sure they will set it up on an 8"x10" layout and trim it to size. Nothing looks worse than an 8 x 10 photo with a resume sticking out around the edges.

Just a few more mundane points. You probably want to get at least 100 resumes printed to start with, depending on the cost and how ambitious you feel. Your resume will change more often than your photo, one hopes, but you don't want to run out of resumes, and the difference in cost between 50 and 100 is usually very little. Attach the resume to the back of the photo either with four little staples, one in each corner, or with a good paper cement, dabbing the corners and edges. Some places will print right on the back of the photo, but then when you want to change the resume you'll have to add another sheet onto the back anyway, so what's the point? However, you do want to have your name on your photo in case they become separated, as I mentioned earlier—if it's not printed on front of the photo, stamp it on the back. Pet peeves of someone who handles stacks and stacks of resumes: resumes that are bigger than the photos; resumes that come off or are only paper clipped onto the photo; resumes that are stapled only once or twice instead of in all 4 corners. Sounds petty, but the loose resume is the one that gets lost or crumpled or eaten by the casting director's puppy.

Mailing out Picture/Resumes

Many of the other "how to be an actor" books that are out there deal at length with different ways to approach agents and casting people, so we won't dwell on something that is really beyond the scope of this book. But I did want to give at least passing mention to the process of mailing out P/R's, since that's a bugaboo for many well-intentioned actors.

In addition to the P/R's that you'll take with you on auditions, you'll want to mail a bunch out to try to get more auditions. Here's what you need to start making your P/R work for you:

- 100 photos that you love and that look like you, back from the copy service.
- 100 newly composed and compellingly laid-out resumes.
- 100 or more Postcards that you have had made from the most appropriate of your photos.
- A list of your targets, whether agents, casting directors, artistic directors or all of the above.
- Attractive, businesslike (not necessarily expensive) stationery for your cover letters and paper clips to attach them to P/R's.
- Large envelopes to hold P/R's and cover letter, and postage for same. [Note: it is *not* necessary to use a cardboard insert when mailing a P/R; it's not worth the expense or the trees.]
- A means of writing the cover letters, whether that's a service, your own computer, a typewriter or a pen.
- *Time and commitment* to get the letters written and mailed.

First we'll talk about the letters or cards themselves, then about your procedure for getting them out. Tasteful and businesslike is the key to cover letters, whether hand written or typed. Forget the scented stationery and violet ink you got from Aunt Margaret for Christmas, get a reasonably priced pack of stationery in white or a muted color, in a size smaller than your 8x10, so it doesn't stick out over the edges. (You've noticed by now that I'm big on not letting anything stick out over the edges of your photo. That's because I really hate it when you try to stack a pile of P/R's neatly, or put them in a file, and you can't because there are edges of resumes and cover letters sticking out all over.)

In determining what to say in a cover letter, follow the theme of your P/R: professional and businesslike, but with your own personality coming through. Keep it short and to the point and don't get cute, but at least one sentence should reveal something about who you are. Tell the person exactly what you want: "Please consider me for extra work or under 5" to a soap casting director; "I understand *Crimes of the Heart* will be part of your season and hope you will consider me for the role of Meg" to an Artistic Director. You get the picture. Handwritten cover letters are perfectly acceptable, if your handwriting is attractive and legible, and if you keep it short. Jean Rohn was emphatic on both brevity and politeness when I spoke to her: "A cover letter is not a post-it note that says 'Hey, Babe, how about a job' [it actually happened]. Even in this business we can maintain some sense of decorum and manners." Jean also mentioned that she loves to get postcards periodically from actors after she has their P/R's on file, "but don't put a postcard in an envelope—that's why they're postcards." Use your postcards as notification of a new service number, or a recent job, or letting folks know you're back in town when you've been away, or just a brief reminder that you're still around.

If you have any point of contact with the person on the receiving end, mention it in your cover letter: a friend who's a client of theirs; an actor you know who worked at their company; a show you saw at their theatre. The technological revolution has had its double-edged effect on cover letters, too. Since everyone now has access to computer-generated, personalized letters (or did you really think Ed McMahon hand typed that letter you got from the publishing house sweepstakes?), the best way to make your letter stand out is by mentioning a specific name or production as a contact point.

If you have the help of a computer (with a letter-quality printer!), or an electronic typewriter with a memory, it is not difficult to organize your own system of sending out resumes with cover letters and postcards on a regular basis to a targeted group of theatres, casting directors, agents, etc. Where do you get this targeted group? Work from lists that run in trade papers, various actors' guides available in the major entertainment centers, TV's *Ross Reports*, etc. Lists are available for casting directors in every area of theatre, modeling, film and TV; for theatres with summer or winter seasons; for talent agents and personal managers—just about anyone you would ever need to send a P/R to. See the Appendix for all these resources. If you have your own computer, you can enter lists from any of these sources onto your own data base, and run off labels for specific purposes at any given time; regional theatres in the late summer, for example, or summer stock in March. If you don't have a computer, buying lists pre-printed on peel-off labels can save you the time of writing out the address on each envelope.

For some actors, this point in the process is the greatest stumbling block in their career—sending out P/R's and postcards, keeping track of who should get them, when and how often. There's a company called Shakespeare Theatrical Mailing Service in NYC (although they will service actors anywhere in the country) which was created just to help actors with this process. They will send out letters, P/R's, resumes, flyers, or whatever the client wishes, to any number of selected names on their extensive data bank. Prices vary, depending on the number of pieces sent out, and the frequency of mailings (see Appendix for address). The choice between the do-it-yourself approach and hiring a mailing service should be made after assessing your financial *and* organizational capabilities. The total cost of putting together your own cover letter and sending it out to a list you compile yourself is less than hiring a service to do your mailings for you. The question is, *will you actually do it?* That perfect P/R won't do your career any good sitting in your desk drawer. Unless you're like a friend of mine who once told me, "I used to send out lots of pictures and resumes in the mail, but now I just sit home at my desk and drop them in the wastebasket. I figured I'd cut out the middleman." (He's no longer in the business.)

Parting Advice

Once you've read through this book and studied our examples, I hope the worksheets in the back will help you to achieve your goal of a P/R that you are happy to hand across the table to a casting person. Ultimately, I think that's the most valid gauge of a successful P/R: how do you feel when you give it to someone? If there's a twinge of embarrassment or a clutch of doubt in your stomach, take a long hard look at what you're using and consider how you should change it. You want to feel great about your presentation—handing over your P/R should be a positive moment in your audition because you know your P/R shows the true *you* in your best light.

I have seen so many young actors who spin their wheels for a year or more before they even have a clue as to how to be a businessperson. Coming out of schools which claim to train actors to enter the profession, they may have all the specialized acting skills that three or four years of incredibly hard work can muster, but they are babes in the woods when it comes to setting up a small business, which is what the actor must do. Your business is the marketing of your product, i.e., your persona, talent, charisma, skill, etc. The best product in the world will sit on the shelf forever if no one knows what it can do or where to buy it. Talent and training will enable you to excel in a performance, but talent and training will not get you the role in the first place—for that you must rely on marketing skills and business acumen. If you don't have any, get some. Read more books, take workshops in career development and business skills. ***Get yourself organized, and put in the time needed*** to develop and follow up on contacts, stay aware of what's going on in the industry, make yourself known to the casting people in your city.

Both Tom and I are interested in your comments on this book, so that when the time comes to update it in a few years, we can improve it. You can send them to me in Vermont at my office with American Theatre Works, Inc., P.O. Box 519, Dorset, Vermont 05251. And yes, Tom is still shooting, and available at his studio in NYC (212-924-8276). Good luck, and remember that the ogre across the casting table isn't your enemy; she really *wants* you to be the right person for the role so she can go get some lunch.

Ellen Gwynn
AEA, SAG, AFTRA

Service (212) 456-1234
Voice: Legit Soprano
(2 octave range)

Height: 5'6"
Weight: 135
Hair: Auburn
Eyes: Hazel

Recent Credits

Deathtrap	Myra	Fairfield Dinner Playhouse, CT
Significant Other (premiere)	Alison	Boston Post Road Company, CT
Various commercials, voiceovers		WFOV, Fairfield, CT

I am returning to my profession after a seven-year hiatus, during which I produced little art, but two great children. The following credits are from a former life which I refer to as P.M. (pre-Mom):

New York Theatre

Starting Once More	Cynthia	Manhattan Theatre Club
The Sea Gull	Nina	York Theatre Company
		Ellen Renfield, director

Regional and Stock

The 1940's Radio Hour	Connie	Candlewood Playhouse, CT
Crimes of the Heart	Chick	Peterborough Playhouse, NH
A Christmas Carol	Belle	Missouri Repertory Theatre
The Importance of Being Earnest	Gwendolyn	Delaware Theatre Company
The Fantasticks	Luisa	Red Barn Dinner Theatre, CT

Television and Film

Guiding Light	Day Player	CBS - TV
The Cosby Show	Extra	CBS - TV
Cadillac Man	Pizza Girl	Orion

...plus numerous Commercials & Industrials

Training

Voice: Anna Resnikov, Bill Reed, Alison Black *
Commercial: Weist-Barron – Leslie Simmons, Mark Lefitz
Acting: Morris Carnovsky, Uta Hagen, George Shepard, Michael Howard *
Mime, mask & commedia: Donny Osman. *Dance:* Jerri Garner * (jazz & tap)
National Theatre Inst. O'Neill Center, CT; B.A. Williams College, Williamstown, MA

*still studying with these teachers, *post-Mom!*

Special Skills

Swimming & diving, horseback riding, gourmet cook, can knit and weave, great with animals and kids. Skilled at dialects. Drive standard, automatic, 4WD. Own antique clothing, 40's - 70's, and formal wardrobe.

(Sorry to make you turn the book sideways, but it was the only way to lay these resumes out so you could compare them, without getting them too small.)

Ellen Gwynn's Resumes

A. This is Ellen's first resume upon arriving in New York at age 22.

- She chose a sturdy typeface (Times) and large sizes to give the resume some weight: her name in 24 pt. bold, union information and headings in 14 pt. bold, stats and credits in 13 pt. Sections set off with lines fill it out more, too.
- She has only worked in three places, so she uses subheadings under the theatre section. Thus instead of listing Peterborough or Williams College over and over, she now has a column for directors or noting things like the extent of the tour.
- She lists professional experience first, and includes an understudy credit (u/s) since it was a good role.
- In her college credits she names the professional directors she worked with, and includes her directing/producing experience.
- She lists a student film to let people know she's worked in front of a camera.
- Many of the teachers at the O'Neill are known in New York, so listing them all is a good way to fill out the resume. For dance she lists amount and type only.
- She spells out her dialects and other special skills.

B. This is Ellen's resume about four years later; she's now Equity, SAG and AFTRA.

- A graceful, lighter typeface (Palatino) offers more room on a fuller resume: name is 20 pt. bold, unions 14 pt. bold, headings 13 pt. bold; stats 11 pt., credits 12 pt.; she dropped the lines between sections but set off her name with horizontals.
- She makes her vocal range and ability clear in the stats lines and also with her good musical credits.
- She lists New York theatre first, including her children's theatre credit, since it's with a good company. She has enough credits now to drop her understudy credit.
- She lists all her TV work, including extra; with only one feature film, she keeps the student film on the resume also. She indicates she has done commercials and industrials.
- She lists teachers by area, including some of her teachers from the O'Neill; she lists the O'Neill at the end, along with Williams College.
- She indicates many dialects; wardrobe collection could be appealing for commercials or extra work.
- She's letting us know she's working now, through the "recent credits" box.

C. Ellen stopped her career for seven years and had two kids; now they're in school and she's getting back into gear.

- A heavy typeface (Bookman) fills out the resume: all the type sizes are the same as in B, but the heavier typeface makes them appear larger.
- She lists the work she's done in the last few years first, then a short explanation of the hiatus between that and the rest of the resume.
- The rest is similar to resume B, with a few credits dropped; by highlighting her ongoing studies she indicates that she is a serious professional. Her skills section reflects her life experience.

ELLEN GWYNN
Equity Membership Candidate, Eligible Performer

(212) 792-3345 (machine)
Voice: Soprano

Height: 5'6"
Weight: 130
Hair: Auburn
Eyes: Hazel

THEATRE

New England Touring Theatre
OUR LADY LIBERTY — Ensemble — James Turo, director (6 months, 4 states)

Peterborough Playhouse, Peterborough, New Hampshire
CRIMES OF THE HEART — Chick — Elisabeth Boyer, director
STEEL MAGNOLIAS — Annelle (u/s) — Wendy Forman, director
CHILDREN'S THEATRE — Various roles — 6 different plays, 18 performances

Williams College, Williamstown, Mass.
THE BELLE OF AMHERST — Emily Dickinson — Senior Project, self-produced tour of 4 states
MAJOR BARBARA — Sara — Mark S. Ramont, guest director
THE THREEPENNY OPERA — Jenny Diver — Greg Boyd, guest director
GUYS AND DOLLS — Sarah Brown — Cap & Bells Production
NO EXIT — Director/Producer — Second Stage Production

FILM

NO TURNING BACK — Diana (lead) — SUNY Albany, Dept. of Film & Comm. (Special award, U.S. College Film Festival)

EDUCATION & TRAINING
Peterborough Playhouse, New Hampshire - Apprentice, 1990 Season
National Theatre Institute, O'Neill Theatre Center, Connecticut
Voice: Anna Resnikof, Julia White
Movement: Peter Lobdell, John Wilson
Acting: Steve Stettler, Morris Carnovsky
Dance: 6 years Ballet; 1 year Jazz/Tap
B.A. Williams College, Theatre Major

SPECIAL SKILLS
Dialects (Standard British, Cockney, Scots, North Country, American Southern, Midwest), horseback riding, swimming, diving, driving (standard, automatic, dirt bike), American Sign Language.

Ellen Gwynn
AEA, SAG, AFTRA
Service (212) 456-1234

Height: 5'6"; Weight: 130
Hair: Auburn; Eyes: Hazel

Voice: Legit Soprano
(2 octave range, to high C)

New York Theatre
Starting Once More — Cynthia — Manhattan Theatre Club
The Sea Gull — Nina — York Theatre Company
Rapunzel — Rapunzel — Ellen Renfield, director; Promenade Theatre & Tour
The Bacchae — ensemble — Theatreworks/USA; New Stages Ensemble Company

Regional and Stock
The 1940's Radio Hour — Connie — Candlewood Playhouse, CT
Crimes of the Heart — Chick — Peterborough Playhouse, NH
A Christmas Carol — Belle — Missouri Repertory Theatre
The Importance of Being Ernest — Gwendolyn — Delaware Theatre Company
The Fantasticks — Luisa — Red Barn Dinner Theatre, CT

Television and Film
Guiding Light — Day Player — CBS - TV
The Cosby Show — Extra — CBS - TV
Cadillac Man — Pizza Girl — Orion
No Turning Back — Diana (lead) — SUNY Albany Dept. of Film

Commercials & Industrials
List available upon request.

Training
Voice: Anna Resnikof, Bill Reed, Alison Black
Commercial: Weist-Barron – Leslie Simmons, Mark Lefritz
Acting: Morris Carnovsky, Steve Stettler; HB Studios – Uta Hagen, George Shepard
Dance: Jerri Garner (Jazz & tap)   Mime, mask & commedia: Donny Osman
National Theatre Institute, O'Neill Center, CT.   B.A., Williams College, Williamstown, MA

Special Skills
Dialects (many British, American, European), American Sign Language, swimming & diving, horseback riding, gourmet cook. Drive standard & automatic; own 40's & 50's clothes and formal wardrobe.

Recent Credits:

Height: 5'11"
Weight: 165 lbs.
Hair: Black
Eyes: Brown

SAM LAWRENCE CLOVER
AEA, SAG, AFTRA

Actors' Agents, Inc.
1650 Broadway, suite 1513, NYC 10019
Contact: Jeanne Liszt - (212) 727-6334

Sam Lawrence Clover has appeared on Broadway in ONCE ON THIS ISLAND and as Richie in A CHORUS LINE. His film appearances include Zeffirelli's HAMLET with Mel Gibson; KINDERGARTEN COP (Universal); and a tap-dancing role in THE COTTON CLUB. Television roles include the CBS-TV movie WOMEN AT WEST POINT as well as ABC's ALL MY CHILDREN and ONE LIFE TO LIVE. He also appeared as James Little, a recurring role in SEARCH FOR TOMORROW. Additional theatre roles include Joe in SHOWBOAT at Starlight Musicals, Kansas City, Judas in JESUS CHRIST, SUPERSTAR at Artpark in Buffalo, NY; Phil in THAT CHAMPIONSHIP SEASON at Philadelphia Drama Guild, Jimmy in BLUES FOR MR. CHARLIE at the Hudson Guild, NYC and Russell in ZOOMAN AND THE SIGN at the New Federal Theatre, NYC.

Mr. Clover trained at the University of Virginia and received his M.F.A. from the Professional Training Program at Mason Gross School of the Arts, Rutgers University. He has studied acting with Aaron Frankel, William Esper and Katheryn Gately; voice with Kristin Linklater and dance (jazz and tap) with Thommie Walsh, Michael Bennett and Honi Cole. He is certified in Stage Combat by S.A.F.D.; he plays jazz piano; is skilled at swimming, acrobatics and gymnastics; drives standard, automatic and motorcycles.

Sam Lawrence Clover's Resumes

D. This is Sam's New York resume.

• Sam liked the clean, contemporary look of Avant Garde Gothic typeface; name is in 20 pt. bold, set off with *dingbats* (yes, that's what printers actually call various funky little symbols); 14 pt. headings; stats are 11 pt. and credits 12 pt. with titles italicized.

• Sam stresses his "triple threat" talents under his name, rather than unions (with his credits, it's obvious he belongs to all 3 unions). Contact is his agent.

• He lists his Broadway credits separately to make them stand out, then other theatre, film and TV. The better known directors are named.

• He's trained with some top people, so those are the only names he lists, adding his degrees at the end.

• Special skills are simple, straightforward.

E. This is Sam's L.A. resume; his agency is now "bicoastal" and he's being submitted in both cities.

• The typeface is Helvetica, with his name in 28 pt., underlined. Headings are flushleft, with lines for visual interest and clarity. Stats are 13 pt., credits 12 pt.

• Phone numbers for agency offices in both NYC and L.A. are listed.

• Film and TV credits are listed first; Broadway set off from other theatre credits. Caps instead of italics set off names of films, tv, theatre. This reflects a sense that L.A. casting people are interested first in the "project", then in the role and producer.

[Notice that D and E have virtually the same content, but each has a different emphasis and graphic image.]

F. This is an example of a "paragraph style" resume.

• Sam's new agency has a standard format for all their clients' resumes, and has them printed them on the agency's letterhead.

• The resume is typed on an IBM typewriter, in "Courier" typeface (10 pt.), with the name centered, boldfaced and underlined.

• Vital statistics are set off to one side at the top of the resume.

• The paragraph reads like a program bio, with titles in caps. Only the most important roles are mentioned by name, mostly in theatre work. His recurring role in a soap is pointed out. Broadway credits are listed first, being the most impressive; then film, tv and the rest of his theatre work.

• Sam's training and special skills are listed in a separate paragraph, to make them a little easier to read. This section could also be reduced to a simple listing of training programs attended, but because his teachers are so recognizable, they're mentioned by name.

❖ Sam Lawrence Clover ❖

Actor/Singer/Dancer

AEA, SAG, AFTRA
Baritone/Tenor
Contact: **Franklin Artists**
(212) 745-8800

Height: 5'11"
Weight: 165
Hair: Black
Eyes: Brown

Broadway

Once on this Island	Armand	Booth Theatre
A Chorus Line	Richie	dir: Michael Bennett/Shubert Theatre

Off-Broadway, Regional & Stock

That Championship Season	Phil	Philadelphia Drama Guild
Blues for Mr. Charlie	Jimmy	The Hudson Guild
Zooman and the Sign	Russell	dir: W. King, Jr./New Federal Theatre
Jesus Christ, Superstar	Judas	dir: Peter Sellers/Pepsico Festival
Twelfth Night	Malvolio	North Carolina Shakespeare Festival
Showboat	Joe	Starlight Musicals, Kansas City
Babes in Toyland	Rodrigo	dir: Susan Lawless/Sharon Playhouse

Film

Hamlet	A Player	Icon/Zeffirelli
Kindergarten Cop	Schoolteacher	Universal
The Cotton Club	Johnson	Total Independent, Ltd.
Fort Apache, The Bronx	Police Sergeant	Time-Life

Television

Search For Tomorrow	James Little (Recurring Role)	NBC-TV
Women at West Point	Cadet	CBS-TV
All My Children	Day Player	ABC-TV
One Life to Live	Surgeon	ABC-TV

Commercials & Industrials - List on request.

Training

Acting: Aaron Frankel, William Esper, Katheryn Gately
Voice: Kristin Linklater
Dance: Tap/Jazz with Thommie Walsh, Michael Bennett, Honi Cole
Stage Combat: Richard Sordelet (S.A.F.D. certified)
M.F.A. Mason Gross School of the Arts, Rutgers University; B.F.A. University of Viginia

Special Skills

Drive any vehicle. Gymnastics, acrobatics, swimming. Play jazz piano.

SAM LAWRENCE CLOVER

AEA, SAG, AFTRA
Contact: **Franklin Artists**
L.A. (213) 833-2825; N.Y. (212) 745-8800

Film

HAMLET	A Player	Icon/Zeffirelli
KINDERGARTEN COP	Schoolteacher	Universal
THE COTTON CLUB	Johnson	Total Independent, Ltd.
FORT APACHE, THE BRONX	Police Sergeant	Time-Life

Television

SEARCH FOR TOMORROW	James Little (Recurring Role)	NBC-TV
WOMEN AT WEST POINT	Cadet	CBS-TV
ALL MY CHILDREN	Day Player	ABC-TV
ONE LIFE TO LIVE	Surgeon	ABC-TV

COMMERCIALS & INDUSTRIALS - List on request.

Theatre

Broadway:

ONCE ON THIS ISLAND	Armand	Booth Theatre
A CHORUS LINE	Richie	Shubert Theatre

Off-Broadway, Regional & Stock:

THAT CHAMPIONSHIP SEASON	Phil	Philadelphia Drama Guild
BLUES FOR MR. CHARLIE	Jimmy	The Hudson Guild, NYC
ZOOMAN AND THE SIGN	Russell	New Federal Theatre, NYC
JESUS CHRIST, SUPERSTAR	Judas	Artpark, Buffalo, NY
TWELFTH NIGHT	Malvolio	North Carolina Shakespeare Festival
SHOWBOAT	Joe	Starlight Musicals, Kansas City

Training

ACTING: Aaron Frankel, William Esper, Katheryn Gately
VOICE: Kristin Linklater
DANCE: Tap/Jazz with Thommie Walsh, Michael Bennett, Honi Cole
STAGE COMBAT: Richard Sordelet (S.A.F.D. certified)
M.F.A. Mason Gross School of the Arts, Rutgers University; B.F.A. University of Viginia

Special Skills

Drive any vehicle. Gymnastics, acrobatics, swimming. Play jazz piano.

Use this page for a rough draft of your resume:

Worksheet #1 - Planning Schedule

(Allot 1-2 weeks each for I and II; III will be determined by photographer's schedule)

Project Start Date:_____ **Finish Date:**_____

I. Research   Time Period: from _____ to _____

Get together with these people to see their P/R *(check off when done)*:

Name   *Phone #*

- ☐ _____
- ☐ _____
- ☐ _____
- ☐ Check out ads in _____
- ☐ Check out yellow pages.

List of photographers *(check each off as you fill out Worksheet #2)*:

Name   *Studio Address*   *Phone*

- ☐ _____
- ☐ _____
- ☐ _____
- ☐ _____
- ☐ _____
- ☐ _____
- ☐ _____
- ☐ _____
- ☐ _____
- ☐ _____

List of copy services *(check each off as you fill out Worksheet #3)*:

Name   *Address*   *Phone*

- ☐ _____
- ☐ _____
- ☐ _____
- ☐ _____
- ☐ _____
- ☐ _____
- ☐ _____
- ☐ _____
- ☐ _____
- ☐ _____

Style(s) of photo selected: _____

Photographer selected: _____

Copy service selected: Photo_____ Resume_____

Cost: Need $_____ in hand by _____

Date and Time of Photo Session: _____

II. Preparation

Time Period: from _____ to _____

☐ Look at P/R's from _____'s files.
☐ Make up rough draft of resume.
☐ Watch commercials and soaps, noticing "types".

Legit shot:

Comments, concept: _____
_____
_____
_____

Ideas for clothing, hair, make-up: _____
_____
_____
_____

Ideas for action at session: _____
_____
_____
_____

Commercial shot:

Comments, concept: _____
_____
_____
_____

Ideas for clothing, hair, make-up: _____
_____
_____
_____

Ideas for action at session: _____
_____
_____
_____

Soap shot:

Comments, concept: _____
_____
_____
_____

Ideas for clothing, hair, make-up: _____
_____
_____
_____

Ideas for action at session: _____
_____
_____
_____

Planning Schedule, Page 2

☐ Take to the photo session:

Clothing: _____
_____
_____
_____
_____

Accessories: _____
_____
_____
_____

Hair/Make-up needs: _____
_____
_____
_____
_____

III. Finished Product

Time Period: from _____ to _____

Pick up contact sheet on _____.
Select best shots by _____.
Show contact sheet and resume draft to:
☐ _____
☐ _____
☐ _____
Take selections to photographer by _____.
Arrangements for retouching: _____
_____
_____

Pick up original print by _____.
Arrangements for copy negative (test print?): _____
_____
_____

Pick up copies of photo & postcard by _____.
Take resume to service by _____.
Pick up copies of resume by _____.

Planning Schedule, Page 3

Use this page for more notes:

Worksheet #2 - Photographer Comparison

Name: _____

Studio Address: _____

Telephone: _____ Date of call/visit: _____

Recommended by: _____

Overall Rating:
- ❏ Strong
- ❏ Average
- ❏ Weak

To figure total cost, carry over applicable charges to column at right.

Shooting fee: ❶ $_____ includes _____ rolls of film, _____ finished prints.

How far in advance must I book? _____

Do you require a deposit? _____

Is there a cancellation fee? _____

Can you arrange for hair & make-up? ❏ yes ❏ no

Cost for hair & make-up? ❷ $_____

How many changes do you allow? _____

Does your stylist alter hair & makeup with changes? _____

How long will the session last? _____

Will you be working with me alone? _____

What style (headshot, bordered, full body) do you prefer/recommend?

_____

How soon can I see the proof sheets? _____

Is there a guarantee? _____

Is there a charge for reshooting? _____

Negative is owned by ❏ me ❏ photographer

How soon can I have the final prints? _____

Who does your retouching? _____

What does it cost? ❸ $_____

Do you make your own reproduction prints? ❏ yes ❏ no

If not, whom do you recommend? _____

What will it cost? ❹ $_____

How much do you charge for extra prints? ❺ $_____

Do you offer a discount if I return for my next set of photos? _____

Other questions, comments: _____

_____

_____

Cost:
- ❶ $_____
- ❷ $_____
- ❸ $_____
- ❹ $_____
- ❺ $_____

$_____
Total

Looking at the Portfolio:

Great	OK	Poor	
❏	❏	❏	Skin tones (skin texture) should be real, not airbrushed or retouched, and not grainy.
❏	❏	❏	Lighting and contrast should separate the face and hair from the background color.
❏	❏	❏	Cropping: If headshot, eyes close to center of picture, head more than 1/2 picture size.
❏	❏	❏	Lighting should be even, soft, like a slightly overcast day, or light through a skylight.
❏	❏	❏	No sharp shadow lines; no place on the face is in such dark shadow that it's obscured.
❏	❏	❏	Neither clothing nor background (esp. in outdoor shot) should distract or pull focus.
❏	❏	❏	Subject's focus should be with eyes into the camera.
❏	❏	❏	Are the eyes "working"? Do they have life?
❏	❏	❏	Pictures should look different from each other.
❏	❏	❏	Overall impression of the book.

Comments: _____

_____

Worksheet #3 – Copy Service Comparison

Name: _____

Address: _____

Telephone: _____ Date of call/visit: _____

Recommended by: _____

Services available: ❑ Photos   ❑ Postcards   ❑ Resumes

Write the cost of various options available in the first column. Decide which options you want, and carry only those into the second column. Then add the second column for your total cost if you choose this service.

Photos:

Basic cost: $_____ per _____ $_____

Additional costs: Test print $_____   _____

Name on front $_____   _____

Rush service $_____   _____

Other _____ $_____   _____

Notes: _____

_____

_____

Postcards:

Basic cost: $_____ per _____ $_____

Additional costs: Second photo $_____   _____

Name on front $_____   _____

Rush service $_____   _____

Other _____ $_____   _____

Notes: _____

_____

_____

Resumes:

Basic cost: $_____ per _____ $_____

Additional costs: Special paper stock $_____   _____

Trim to 8" x 10" $_____   _____

Staple to photo $_____   _____

Print on back of photo $_____   _____

Rush Service $_____   _____

Charge for storage on disk $_____   _____

Charge for update $_____   _____

Other _____ $_____   _____

Typefaces available: _____

_____

Notes: _____

_____

_____

TOTAL $_____

Appendices

A. Glossary of Printing and Photography Terms Used in this Book

Ascender In type, the part of a lower case letter that extends above the body of the letter, as in b, d, f, h, k, l, t.

Bleed A photo that has no white border around the edges is one that "bleeds."

Boldface A heavier or thicker version of a particular typeface.

Book Portfolio containing examples of the work of a photographer, reproduction lab, make-up or retouch artist.

Composite A sheet of photos (usually 4 or more) of an actor in various poses, situations, and dress, used mainly for commercial submissions.

Composition The elements which make up a graphic, including photos, line art, typefaces, spacing, etc.

Contrast Relative difference between light and dark tones in a print. Too much, or "hard," contrast moves the dark tones toward black and the light tones toward white. Too little, or "soft," contrast produces dull grays. Proper contrast maintains pleasing and natural difference among tones.

Copy Negative (or *Reproduction*, or *Inter-Negative*) A large negative (usually 8x10 or 5x7) made by the reproduction lab from the finished print. This large negative is then is used to make less expensive reproduction copies.

Cropping The elimination of unnecessary portions of the photo. The photographer follows cropping directions marked on the proof sheet when enlarging photos.

Descender In type, the part of a lower case letter that extends below the body, as in g, j, p, q, y.

Dingbats A typeface consisting of funky symbols, like ☆ ❖ ❧ ☀ ✆ ✿

Fast/Slow Film The ability of a type of film to gather more light (fast) or less (slow), in order to take advantage of varying light conditions.

Grain Tiny specks which make up the structure of black and white film, and which are visible in the print. The size of grain varies according to the speed of the film (see *Fast/Slow Film*, above). Headshots look best with the smallest grain, hence the slowest film possible.

Headshot A theatrical photograph of an actor from the neckline up; also used as a general term for any theatrical photo or picture/resume.

Italic A slanted version of a particular typeface.

Knockout Type that is set within a white box so it shows up against a dark background.

L.A. style	Borderless photo showing head and torso or full body, usually shot outdoors.
Layout	The visual look of a page, taking into account white space, blocks of copy, headlines, etc.
Legit	Abbreviation for "legitimate theatre." A legit photo is used for theatre and film auditions as opposed to commercial or soap photos.
Look	In this book, referring to the various sides an actor shows of him/herself in a photograph, and the uses these photos are put to, as in "commercial upscale look," etc.
Loupe	Small magnifier used to inspect proof sheet images.
Negative	Processed film from the photo session which contains the image of the photo in reverse. Prints are made by shining light through the negative onto the photographic paper, for varying degrees of enlargement.
Point	Type size is measured in points: 72 points = 1 inch. "12 point type" means the distance from the top of the ascender to the bottom of the descender (top of a "k" to bottom of a "y") is 1/6 of an inch.
Portrait	A style of theatrical photo featuring a wide white border around the image; usually shows head and at least part of the torso.
Proof Sheet	A sheet containing all the images recorded on one roll of film. These images are the actual size of the negative used.
Retouching	Altering the image by removing or adding to the surface of the finished print. There are two methods: *Etching*, which is the gradual removal of emulsion on the print surface with a sharp knife to produce progressively lighter tones, and *Airbrushing*, in which a fine spray of paint or dye is applied to the surface of the print.
Reverse	Type that is printed in white on a black background is "reverse" type.
Serif	Small counter strokes that "finish off" the ends of the body strokes of a letter. A typeface may be "serif" or "sans serif", i.e. with or without serifs.
Skin Tone	Relative lightness or darkness of skin in a finished print. Proper tone suggests the natural texture of living skin.
Stock	The kind of paper used by a printer; paper stock comes in various weights, colors, and finishes.
Style	The overall appearance of a theatrical photo, determined by such factors as its being shot outdoors or in a studio, showing head alone or head and partial body, printed with or without a border, etc.
Subtext	In this book, referring to the inner dialogue an actor carries on to keep a photo session active and vital.
Type	A general category used by casting people to communicate how a particular actor would normally be cast, or what kind of actor is needed for a given role.
Typeface	The shape, weight and "look" of a particular style of type, referred to by copyrighted names such as "Times Roman", "Helvetica," etc.
Upscale	A more sophisticated commercial photo, portraying the actor as an executive or business person.

B. Resources

*Service Organizations: Those marked * sponsor annual combined auditions.*

Alternate ROOTS *1083 Austin Ave., Atlanta, GA 30307 (404) 577-1079*

Alliance of Resident Theatres/New York (ART/NY) *131 Varick St. #904, NYC10013*
   (212) 989-5257

Florida Professional Theatres Association (FPTA)* *P.O. Box 2922, West Palm Beach, FL 33402*
   (407) 848-6231

Indiana Theatre Association (INTA)* *c/o Linda Charbonneau, Butler University Theatre,*
   4600 Sunset Ave., Indianapolis, IN 46208

Institute of Outdoor Drama* *CB#3240, NationsBank Plaza, Chapel Hill, NC 27599-3240*
   (919) 962-1328

League of Washington (D.C.) Theatres (LWT)* *410 8th St., NW, suite 600, Wash., D.C. 20004*
   (202) 638-4270

LORT (League of Resident Theatres) Lottery Auditions* *AEA Audition Center, 165 W. 46th St.,*
   NYC 10036 (212) 869-8530

Mid-America Theatre Conference (MATC)* *c/o Glenn Q. Pierce, 6514 W. 89th, apt. 121, Overland*
   Park, KS 66212 (913) 648-2378

National Dinner Theatre Association (NDTA)* *P.O. Box 726, Marshall, MI 49068 (616) 781-7859*

New England Theatre Conference (NETC)* *c/o Northeastern Univ. Dept. of Theatre,*
   360 Huntington Ave., Boston, MA 02115 (617) 893-3120

Ohio Theatre Alliance (OTA)* *61 Jefferson Ave., Columbus, OH 43215 (614) 228-1998*

Southeast Theatre Conference (SETC)* *Marian Smith, P.O. Box 9868, UNC, Greensboro,*
   NC 27429-0868

Society for Theatrical Artists' Guidance & Enhancement (STAGE) *P.O. Box 214820, Dallas,*
   TX 75221 (214) 559-3917

StageSource *88 Tremont St., suite #714, Boston, MA 02108 (617) 720-6066*

Theatre Bay Area (TBA)* *657 Mission St., suite 402, San Francisco, CA 94105 (415) 957-1557*

University/Resident Theatre Association (U/RTA)* *1560 Broadway, Suite 903, New York,*
   NY 10036 (212) 221-1130

Various Casting Aids

Academy Players Directory *Academy of Motion Pictures, 8949 Wilshire Blvd, Beverly Hills, CA*
   90211 (310) 247-3000 This is a compilation of headshots, representations, and/or service contracts
   for performers, published 3 times a year. To be listed you must be a member of one of the 4A's
   (AEA, SAG, AFTRA, AGVA), or have a SAG franchised agent. Write for information.

AEA Hotlines Cities which have 100+ Equity members have an Equity Liaison assigned to them, and
   run an Equity Hotline, a phone number you can call for information on upcoming auditions. Call
   your AEA branch office for the AEA Liason or Hotline in your city.

American Theatre Magazine *c/o TCG, 355 Lexington Ave., New York, NY 10017 (212) 697-5230*
   Monthly magazine of professional non-profit theatres with schedule of productions of member
   theatres; October issue lists full season schedule of TCG member theatres.

Audition News *6272 W. North Ave., Chicago, IL 60639 (312) 637-4695* Monthly; Chicago & mid-
   west casting notices for music, theatre, dance, variety, modeling.

Back Stage Publications *P.O. Box 5017, Brentwood, TN, 37024 1-800-999-3322* Weekly trade paper
   with audition notices for NYC & regional theatre, stock, film. On newsstands near NYC, or by subscription.

Call Board *657 Mission St., ste. #402, San Francisco, CA 94103 (415) 957-5577* Monthly publication
   of Theatre Bay Area, covering theatre news and audition notices.

Chicago Reader *11 E. Illinois, Chicago, IL 60611 (312) 828-0350* Weekly newspaper with complete entertainment section for Chicago area, including casting notices.

L.A. Drama-Logue *1456 N. Gordon, Hollywood, CA 90028 (213) 464-5079* Weekly trade paper published in Hollywood, with L.A. and national audition notices.

Mailing Labels: You can buy mailing lists on peel-off labels for agents, directors and casting directors in theatre, TV, commercials, film, etc. through most drama specialty bookstores or directly from **Hendersons** (360 E. 65th St., #15E, NYC 10021), **Peter Glenn Publications** (42 W. 38th St., #802, NYC 10018) or **Up-To-Date Casting Labels** (449 W. 44th St., #3S, NYC 10036).

New England Casting News *P.O. Box 201, Boston, MA 02134 (617) 787-2991* Bimonthly listing of auditions for New England. Acting & staff job openings.

New England Entertainment Digest (NEED) *P.O. Box 313, Portland, CT 06480 (203) 342-4730* Bimonthly newspaper covering Boston and New England area; audition notices and news on theatre, film, dance, music & arts in general.

New York Casting *110 Greene St., suite 800, NYC 10012 (212) 334-6700* Weekly NY casting paper

Theatrical Index *888 Eighth Ave., NYC 10019. (212) 586-6343* Listing of shows in production or development, in NY and regional theatres. Also lists of agents & producers.

Performink *3223 N Sheffield, 3rd Fl., Chicago, IL 60657 (312) 296-4600* Chicago's bi-weekly theatre news journal. Articles by & for working theatre professionals. Includes audition notices & classified ads.

Players Guide *165 West 46th St., Suite 1305, NYC 10036. (212) 869-3570* Similar to Academy Players Directory for NYC. Must be member of AEA, AFTRA, or SAG. Write for information.

Ross Reports *Television Index, Inc. 40-29 27th St., L.I.City, NY 11101 (718) 937-3990* Monthly list of casting people, franchised agents with commercial casting in NY area, unions, literary agents, NY ad agencies, casting in soaps (NY & LA), TV packagers, all prime-time network programming and production personnel.

Shakespeare Theatrical Mailing Service *311 W. 43rd St., 2nd Fl., NYC 10036 (212) 956-6245* Although based in NYC, they will handle requests from anywhere to mail your P/R's, cover letters, flyers, postcards, etc., to their mailing lists or your own.

Show Business *1501 Broadway, New York, NY 10036 (212) 354-7600* Weekly NY trade paper, audition notices, on newsstands in NYC & Phila. or by subscription.

Theatrical Calendar *Celebrity Svc. Int'l., 1780 B'way, #300, NYC 10019 (212) 757-7979* Published twice a month, lists on & off-Broadway and regional productions; producers, contacts, schedules, etc.

Variety *P.O. Box 710, Brewster, NY 10509-9864* and **Daily Variety** *P.O. Box 7550, Torrance, CA 90504 1-800-552-3632.* Weekly in NY, Daily in L.A.; news, casting and financial information on entertainment industry.

Drama Specialty Bookstores Around The Country

EASTERN STATES:

Actors' Heritage *262 West 44th St., New York, NY 10036 (212) 944-7490*

Actors Too *210 West 45th St., NYC, NY 10036 (212) 382-0577*

Applause Theatre And Cinema Books *211 West 71st St. (W of B'way, lower level) New York, NY 10023; FAX (212) 721-2856; Phone (212) 496-7511*

Backstage, Inc. *2101 P Street, NW, Washington, D.C. 20037 (202) 775-1488*

Baker's Plays *100 Chauncy Street, Boston, MA 02111 (617) 482-1280*

Drama Book Shop *723 Seventh Ave., New York, NY 10019 (212) 944-0595*

INTERMISSION: The Shop for the Performing Arts *8405 Germantown Ave., Philadelphia, PA 19118 (215) 242-8515*

Samuel French, Inc. *45 West 25th St., New York, NY 10010 (212) 206-8990*

Theatre Connection *264J McLaws Circle, Williamsburg, VA 23185 (804) 221-0907*

MID-WEST:

Act I Bookstore *2632 North Lincoln, Chicago, IL 60614 (312) 348-6757*

Scenes *3168 North Clark, Chicago, IL 60657 (312) 525-1007*

WESTERN STATES:

Cinema Books *4753 Roosevelt Way N.E., Seattle, WA 98105 (206) 547-7667*

Drama Books *134 Ninth Street, San Francisco, CA 94103 (415) 255-0604*

Larry Edmund's Bookstore *6644 Hollywood Blvd., Hollywood, CA 90028 (213) 463-3273*

Limelight Bookstore *1803 Market St., San Francisco, CA 94103 (415) 864-2265*

Samuel French's Theatre and Film Bookshop *7623 Sunset Blvd., Hollywood, CA 90046 (213) 876-0570 11963 Ventura Blvd., Studio City, CA 91604 (818) 762-0535*

Books About Your Acting Career: *You should find these at any of the bookstores above. * indicates most highly recommended in its particular category.*

AGENTS, ETC.

Agents: The Guide to Today's Powerbrokers *Linda Bensky (Paris Publishing, P.O. Box 480825, L.A., CA 90048. 1992.) $14.95*

Everything You Always Wanted To Know About L.A.'S & NY'S Casting Directors . . . But Were Afraid To Ask *Wendy Shawn (Castbusters, P.O. Box 67C75, L.A., CA, 1986. $8.95*

***The L.A. Agent Book: Get the Agent You Need and the Career You Want** K. Callan, (Sweden Press, CA. 1992.) $15.95*

***The NY Agent Book: Get the Agent You Need and the Career You Want** K. Callan (Sweden Press, CA. 1993.) $15.95*

AUDITIONING

***Audition** Michael Shurtleff (Walker & Co., NYC, 1978.) cloth $9.95, pap. $7.95 & small pap. ed. $5.99 (recommended for theatre)*

***The Audition Book** Ed Hooks (Backstage Books/Watson-Guptil, NYC, 1989) $14.95 (recommended for TV/film)*

Auditioning for the Musical Theatre *Fred Silver (Penguin Press, NYC, 1986.) $10.00*

Auditions & Scenes from Shakespeare *Ed. by Joan & Richard Bell (Theatre Directories, Dorset, VT. 1994.) $10.95*

How to Audition *Gordon Hunt (Harper & Row, NYC, 1986.) $11.00*

The Monologue Workshop *Jack Poggi (Applause Acting Series, NYC, 1989.) $10.95*

ACTING CAREER ENHANCEMENT

***Acting Professionally** (4th Ed.) Robert Cohen (Mayfield Pub. Co., Palo Alto, CA, 1990.) $13.95*

The Back Stage Handbook for Performing Artists *Edited & Compiled by Sherry Eaker (Back Stage Publications, 330 W. 42nd St., NYC 10036. 1995.)*

***How to Be a Working Actor** Mari Lyn Henry & Lynne Rogers (M. Evans & Co., NYC, 1986.) $9.95*

How to Make It in Show Biz (A Survival Kit) *June Walker Rogers (Dramatic Publishing Co., Woodstock, IL, 1986.) $12.95*

How to Sell Yourself as an Actor *K. Callan (Sweden Press, Los Angeles, CA.) $12.95*

Word of Mouth *Susan Blu & Molly Ann Mullin (Pomegranate Press, Ltd.) $12.95*

***Your Film Acting Career** M.K. Lewis & Rosemary R. Lewis (Samuel French Trade, CA.) $15.95*

DIRECTORIES & LISTINGS, ETC.

These are guides to the industry, specific to the areas indicated in the titles.

The Actor's Handbook: Seattle & the Pacific Northwest *Ed. Ellen Taft (Capital Hill Press, Seattle, WA. Annual.)*

An Actor's Guide to Agencies in Toronto *Ed. by John Mein (Moonlighters Pub., Toronto)*

The Black Talent Resource Guide *(Lover Child Publishing, Hollywood, CA)*

Chicago Talent Handbook *(Chicago Review Press, 814 North Franklin St., Chicago, IL 60610) (modeling)*

Contact Book *(Celebrity Service Internat'l, 1780 B'way, suite 300, NYC 10019. International, annual.)*

Directory of Theatre Training Programs *Ed. by Jill Charles (Theatre Directories, Dorset, VT. National, biennial.)*

Getting Organized: Theatrical Directory & Datebook Calendar *Gaylyn Britton (Moonlighters Pub., Toronto)*

International Directory of Model & Talent Agencies & Schools *(Peter Glenn Publications, NY)*

The Madison Avenue Handbook *(Peter Glenn Publications, NY. Modeling, annual.)*

NY Casting & Survival Guide...& Datebook *(Peter Glenn Publications, NY Annual.)*

Regional Theatre Directory *Ed. by Jill Charles (Theatre Directories, P.O. Box 519, Dorset, VT. National, annual.)*

The Source: The Greater Boston Theatre Resource Guide *Ed. by Peggy Roberts (StageSource, Boston, MA. Annual.)*

Summer Theatre Directory *Ed. by Jill Charles (Theatre Directories, P.O. Box 519, Dorset, VT. National, annual.)*

Theatre Profiles *(TCG, 355 Lexington Ave., NYC 10017. National, biennial.)*

The Working Actor's Guide - L.A. *(Paul Flattery Productions, P.O. Box 2147, Hollywood, CA 90078. Annual)*